Who's Invited to Share?
Using Literacy to Teach For Equity and Social Justice

Roxanne Henkin

gist of the book-(pg.#118)

HEINEMANN
Portsmouth, NH

HEINEMANN
A division of Reed Elsevier Inc.
361 Hanover Street
Portsmouth, NH 03801-3912

Offices and agents throughout the world

To my parents, and to Mary Lou, with love

CIP is on file at the Library of Congress
ISBN 0-325-00052-2

Editors: Leigh Peake, William Varner
Cover design: Darci Mehall
Manufacturing: Louise Richardson

Printed in the United States of America on acid-free paper.

05   04   03   02   01 VP   2   3   4   5   6

Contents

v   Acknowledgments

Part One   Defining the Problems

1   Introduction

5   Chapter 1 | Who Is Invited to Share?

16   Chapter 2 | What Do We Mean When We Say Diversity?

19   Chapter 3 | Why Is Diversity so Difficult?

25   Chapter 4 | The Worst Thing You Can Call a Boy Is a Girl

31   Chapter 5 | Talk, Diversity, and Gender: Trying to Communicate

Part Two   Searching for Solutions

45   Chapter 6 | What If My Class Is Already Multicultural?

58   Chapter 7 | Talk, Reflection, and Inquiry: Three Key Components of the Literacy Process

67   Chapter 8 | Learning to Hear Each Other

78   Chapter 9 | Who Are the Outsiders?

89   Chapter 10 | The Inclusive Inquiry Cycle

102   Chapter 11 | Using Literacy to Create Social Justice
Classrooms

120   Chapter 12 | What If My Class Is Not Diverse?

128   Chapter 13 | Teaching For Ethics: At School and at Home

137   Chapter 14 | A Final Word

141   Appendix A | *When I Got Shot* By Erick Padilla

145   Appendix B | References

146   Appendix C | Who Is Invited to Share in My Classroom?

147   Appendix D | How Well Do You Know Your Students' Home Lives?

148   Appendix E | Children's Books by Possible Themes

165   Appendix F | Other Resources for Teaching for Social Justice

Acknowledgments

I am grateful to the many wonderful teachers I have talked and worked with, especially over the past two years. There are so many who have contributed, but I want to especially thank Peggy Nadziejko and Mickey Nuccio and their classes. In addition, I want to thank Linda Bailey, Jeff Siddall, Kathy Feldheim, Faith Barbera-Mirza, Carolyn Fabrick, and Lorri Davis for their input. Sue Anderson and Mary Lou Daugherty assisted with the enormous task of compiling the booklists. I also want to thank my editors at Heinemann. Each of them, in their own way, contributed to making this a better book.

I'd also like to thank Cicero, Illinois District 99 for the opportunity to work in the district. I'm only sorry that I don't have the space to name all of the outstanding teachers that I've had the privilege to work with. I'd also like to acknowledge the superintendent, Dr. Anthony Scariano and the assistant superintendent, Dr. Ed Aksamit. Additionally, I want to thank administrators Loretta Tannheimer, Mirjana Skruodys, Bob Cieply, Cindy Mosca, Paty Welegala, Barb Kohut, and Joyce Hodan. I applaud their commitment to holistic literacy, as well as the vision and the hard work of all the Cicero principals and assistant principals.

I have been greatly influenced by the work of Carole Edelsky, Bess Altwerger, Barbara Flores, Elizabeth Saavedra, Linda Christensen, Bob Peterson, Patrick Shannon, and the teachers associated with *Rethinking Schools*. These individuals are our trailbrazers, opening up possibilities and nudging us to go further. I am also indebted to Jerome Harste, Kathy Short, and Carolyn Burke for their generative literacy work, especially the inquiry cycle. My work is based on the inquiry cycle, which I find tremendously useful.

Finally, I'd like to thank my family for their support during the process of writing the book. They've graciously allowed me to tell their stories. I especially want to thank my parents, Audrey and Ed Henkin, and Mary Lou. She provided her support, help, love, and belief in this project. I can't possibly thank you enough.

Introduction

I've spent most of my life as a teacher. Throughout my career, I've been especially concerned about the kids who never seem to fit in. My heart goes out to them.

Danny's Story

Danny was in my class for two years, so I knew him as both a first grader and a second grader. He was a quiet child and difficult to understand. He had a speech problem that further isolated him from the other children. Whenever he tried to speak, the others would tease him and laugh at him. His language problem also complicated his literacy development. He was able to write only fragments of sentences through most of first grade.

Danny also had a balance problem, so he was constantly falling out of his seat. He dropped his pencil countless times each day. During conference, his hands flailed and he accidentally knocked my glasses off my face. When the other children chose teams for kickball, Danny was always the last to be chosen. Perhaps you know a boy like Danny: He's the one standing alone in the playground.

Jeri's Story

Jeri was in my class for two years. When she walked into my first grade classroom, she was the only girl wearing jeans; everyone else wore color-co-ordinated dresses or outfits with matching hair ribbons. Jeri's wild blonde hair flew in every direction. Although her hair had started the day in two ponytails, most of it had escaped the confines of the rubber bands. She was too busy running around to worry about her hair.

Jeri was the only girl who signed up for lunchtime soccer. I admired her spunk and courage. She approached reading and writing the way she ap-proached sports: She knew she could do it. But when the students were given free-choice activities, or allowed to choose whom they would like to work with, Jeri was always left out. The girls didn't invite her into their cir-cle.

It has been many years since I had Jeri in my class. By now, she has grown up and is living her adult life. But that hurt and bewildered look on her face has stayed with me and is as vivid now as it was in the 1970s. I've never forgotten her pain. Over the years I've seen countless children who were outsiders during their school experience. I've thought about how these children often slip through the cracks; they are the ones we educators never reach.

Other Students Speak

As they have grown older, some of these students have been able to help us by telling us in their own words how they felt during their elementary and high school years. Now in college, Dana Szymkowiak recalls her high school experience:

> I would get confused and frustrated at the teachers and then the home-work. I was embarrassed and scared to ask for help. I was made to feel that if I didn't understand, it was because I wasn't paying attention. It was eas-ier to copy someone else's homework than have to do it myself. Graduat-ing from high school came down to my very last final on the last day . . .

Sam, now a sophomore in college, describes his school experience:

> All elementary school and junior high was a pain. I felt like an outsider. I didn't know I had a gift [for art] until high school. I was bilingual. I was in a bilingual group. That's Spanish and English and I kept getting messed up. I was the quiet one in the back. I wouldn't raise my hand. I always felt like an outsider."

As I dedicated my career to the teaching of reading and writing, I became convinced that literacy offers us tremendous vehicles to help not only these children, but all of our students to gain greater understanding and insight into all the peoples of the world. Literacy can serve as a tool to open our worlds and help us to better understand and accept all human beings. This book has been germinating for a long time—for the twenty-five years I have spent in education, first as a teacher and now as a professor of literacy. I'm still in classrooms one or two days a week. Each time I step into a room, I watch carefully. I admire the wonderful teachers and students and administrators. I'm often excited about the book discussions, writing, and inquiry the students are pursuing, whether I'm in a first- or sixth-grade classroom. But always, I am on the lookout, watching who is talking with whom. When there is choice, who is invited to share in a conversation or an activity? Who is left on the outside? I am especially sensitive and on the alert for these children. It is important for me to admit that I wasn't always this way; I didn't always notice. But after the year-long study described in Chapter 1 of this book, I will never be complacent again. There was so much I didn't see, and so much more I still need to learn.

1 | Who Is Invited To Share?

Reading clubs. Writing workshops. Peer conferences. Structures aimed at increasing participation and equity. As teachers, we believe the invitations extended during writing and reading workshops give students many occasions to participate in beneficial literacy experiences. But do they really? Do these structures give all students equal access and opportunities to participate and grow in our classrooms?

Frank Smith (1988) uses the term "literacy club" as a metaphor to describe the community of readers and writers that can develop in a classroom. I have always assumed that literacy clubs are good for students, but that presumes a democratic classroom where membership is both fair and equitable. Is this always the case? Is everyone allowed to join the literacy club? Is there only one literacy club, or are there multiple literacy clubs that occur in classrooms that may both offer and deny membership to children?

I participated in and studied weekly a first–grade writing workshop during the 1991–1992 school year. The focus of the study was on the collaborative culture of the writing workshop and some of the factors that inhibited or enhanced literacy development. The teacher and I were friends and worked together whenever I was present. I conferred with the children, interviewed them, and acted as another facilitator.

The students were mainly from middle–class families in a near-west Chicago suburb. Most of the ten boys and nine girls in the class were Caucasian, while two were of Indian descent, and a third was Hispanic. The data collection included field notes of classroom observations (Bogdan and Biklen 1982), audiotapes and videotapes of writing conferences, and student and teacher interviews (Spradley 1979). Both the classroom teacher and I believed in writing workshops and felt they were beneficial for all students.

I thought that the classroom community was strong and supportive for every child. I discovered that there were several literacy clubs (Myers 1992) operating in the classroom and that as in Lensmire's (1992) study of a third grade class, some students were excluded based on gender and social status.

Gender Issues in Writing Workshop

I had read about gender and equity issues, but assumed that this was a problem for older children, not first–graders. Gender was the distinguishing factor between the major clubs. There was a boys' literacy club and a girls' literacy club. While girls read, wrote, and conferred together, they rarely had conferences with the boys.

The boys and girls worked together when required, but when given the choice, they chose most of the time to work in groups of the same sex. Although our demonstrations modeled boy and girl interactions, this was not an invitation accepted by many students. We assumed that both the boys and the girls were comfortable with this arrangement. Most of the boys were happy with this situation, perceiving that their interests were much different from the girls'. During one of my interviews with a student named Don, he raised the issue.

DON: Well, well I guess I thought that I was the only boy left that would conference with him.

RH: Can you conference with girls? Do boys conference with girls?

DON: Not usually.

SEVERAL BOYS: Yeah!

DON: They don't usually do it, but I know you can.

RASHI (another student): It doesn't matter if boys don't conference.

Several boys: Rashi, Rashi, you're not in on this!

Our discussion continued. Don took my questions seriously and tried to provide reflective answers. He was bright and perceptive, but was functioning at a low level in the classroom during the first part of the year. He had tantrums and difficulty working with his peers. His colored markers were very important to him and seemed to bring him some status. Many of the boys would ask to borrow his markers. However, he wasn't good at sharing and often had fights and/or shed tears over his markers. Don told me that I was asking "hard questions" about conferences. The boys were hard-pressed to explain why they didn't conference with the girls.

PAUL: I don't know.

ALAN: 'Cause they are girls.

JON: 'Cause the girls don't know, you know if it's on sports. Well, they don't really. Well, we probably know more about sports and, yeah, you know what I mean.

PAUL: I think it's just a habit and I, um, and like, I, um, was doing an inventor story and all that, I asked some of the boys and they knew more about it and I asked some of the girls and they didn't.

Paul did seem to be the exception to the rule. Both the boys and the girls said that Paul needed a lot of conferences and would ask girls for conferences, too. I was interviewing Paul, but all of the boys in the class gravitated to our table and joined in the discussion. Although none of the girls came near, they listened from around the room. The boys agreed that the problem was that girls didn't know much about what they were interested in. Even when confronted with contradictory evidence, the boys remained firm that the girls could not help them. The boys acknowledged that although one girl did write about something interesting, she was still viewed as an inadequate partner.

MARTY: Yeah, yeah like Sarah was writing a story on Lance Johnson and Bo Jackson.

BART: Sarah? Yeah, right Sarah.

MARTY: And I tried to get a couple of boys and they said, gave me like a couple of sentences and when I asked one of the girls, they just said, um well.

The way the boys saw it, girls were simply not adequate partners, and they held to this view even when girls were writing about sports.

RH: All right, let's say you guys aren't writing about sports. Let's say that you're writing about something else.

Bart: Well.

Paul: Like space.

Alan: Planets.

Paul: Then we still, if we still ask the girls then they would say, um, "I don't really know much about space."

Bart: Especially Terminator.

Paul: Yeah.

Bart: Terminator.

Marty: Stuff like that. Stuff like the boys like to write.

RH: Is there anything that the boys like to write about that the girls know about?

(In unison): No.

Paul: It's like, whatever the girls like to write about, the boys don't know.

Bart: Well, some girls know about space.

RH: So the boys don't know what the girls like to write about?

Bart: Yeah, 'cause like; Erin was just writing a story about a baby, and her hardcover was about a prince and a princess and stuff like that.

Alan: And the prince and the princess—

RH: And you guys don't know about babies?

Paul: Yeah, we don't really like to tell.

(Boys in unison): Yeah, yeah.

Paul: It's just that we don't really like those kind of stories.

Bart: Yeah, those kind of stories.

Paul: We like science.

RH: Wait a second Marty, you have a baby sister. Don't you like to write about your baby sister?

Marty: Well, I never really thought about that.

BART: He dedicates a lot of books to her, doesn't you Marty?

RH: But you haven't written about her? How come?

Marty: I don't know.

The boys listed and discussed reasonable writing topics. Topics not deemed appropriate also appeared to be clear to the boys, but more difficult to explain. Writing about babies was the territory of the girls, and therefore forbidden to the boys. The girls watched silently as the boys listed the reasons why girls made poor conference partners. None of them approached the boys or challenged their statements.

The following week, I asked the girls the same questions. The boys couldn't contain themselves and converged as a group to challenge the girls' responses. I had to ask the boys to sit down and let the girls speak for themselves. When asked to discuss boy/girl conferences and topics, some of the girls were surprisingly articulate.

RH: Do you ever ask boys for a conference?

GIRLS: (in unison) No.

ERIN: I think I did one time.

JANE: I was thinking about doing that one time, but then I went to a girl first and I'm like, if this girl doesn't say yes, I'm going to the boys and she said yes.

RH: Well, why do you go to the girls first for a conference?

JANE: 'Cause I think they'd say yes more than the boys.

ERIN: Yeah, because.

JANE: 'Cause boys hardly say yes to me on anything.

Jane and Erin were two of the children I had chosen to interview on a weekly basis because of their low reading levels at the beginning of the year. During the last exchange, Jane began to answer even before I finished my question. Erin was also speaking simultaneously, providing support for Jean. This dueting (Falk 1979) provided a kind of scaffolding (Bruner 1978) for each other that allowed them to continue thinking about complicated issues for a sustained period of time.

ERIN: Yeah, they probably don't say yes because they always have conferences with boys because boys, you know, don't very like, hang with girls a lot and play with them.

RH: Why do you think the boys say no to you?

ERIN: Because they don't like girls or something.

RH: So you think they say no because they don't like girls?

ERIN: Or because—

JANE: They're laughing at us.

Again, Erin and Jane are supporting each other. Thinking together, they identify two possible reasons why the boys may be excluding them.

RH: Why do you think the boys don't want to conference with the girls?

ERIN: Because maybe they really like girls but they don't want to show it.

JANE: Yeah, and they're afraid to show it. And just because we're something else. Just because we're females, probably. We can't help it that we're females.

Erin and Jane jointly handle one end of the discussion. Jane repeats, "They're afraid to show it," and then moves on to her deeper analysis. It's possible that without Erin's support, she would not have made these connections. The next interchange is marked by pauses providing wait time as they continue to ponder these questions.

RH: Why do you think boys are afraid to show they like girls?

ERIN: Um, because maybe I don't . . .

JANE: You got me on that.

JANE: Maybe because like, they um, maybe 'cause boys, the boys laughed at me because Bart kind of likes me and he went to my house, but now I think he doesn't like me that much cause he said, "Jane has a lot of Barbies," and all the boys laughed. Maybe because we have like toys like Barbies and they have other things.

NANCY: They have G.I. Joes or something like that.

JANE: Uh huh.

NANCY: Batman.

RH: So it's the kind of toys you have that make boys not like you?

ERIN: Well, because they don't like very much of the girl stuff. Alan, he doesn't mind the girl stuff and I don't mind his boy stuff.

JANE: I don't mind boy stuff.

RH: You don't mind boy stuff, Jane?

JANE: But I do mind guns because my mom doesn't like guns and I don't either. My mom likes water guns, that's what I like, but no other guns.

The girls were trying to understand why the boys didn't choose them. For the boys, this was a pragmatic issue, the girls simply couldn't provide what they needed. But for the girls, the rejection was puzzling, something they struggled to articulate and understand.

RH: What is the reason that you pick boys?

Nancy: Um.

JANE: My reason is they're more with girls. Girls are more with girls.

RH: I don't understand, what do you mean, girls are more with girls?

JANE: 'Cause we're the same things and boys are the same things, but I still wonder why no boys never pick a girl.

I was having difficulty understanding what Jane meant, so I asked her again.

RH: What do you mean girls pick girls are the same thing?

JANE: Well, 'cause girls and girls are both girls.

Jane used the same words to try to explain. Perhaps she was trying to explain a concept that she had never verbalized before. Even though I had trouble following, Erin seemed to understand and encourage her. Jane had difficulty explaining this concept, but it was central to her next point.

JANE: Yeah. Like girls and boys, that's what I mean.

ERIN: And that's why I like boys and girls.

JANE: I do too. Same with white people liking black people.

ERIN: Yeah, and brown people.

RH: What do you mean?

JANE: Well, like some people, it's like boys and girls don't like each other. It's just like white people and brown people don't like each other sometimes.

RH: And does that make sense?

JANE: Uh. Everyone should like each other.

RH: How can we make everybody like each other?

ERIN: Well, when we have conferences.

JANE: I don't think we can make the guys.

This was a significant discussion for both Jane and Erin. They were thinking together, pushing themselves to consider new ideas and to forge new connections. Their joint thinking was complementary; spurring and inspiring each other to move forward conceptually. Although this was an interesting topic for the boys to discuss, it was clearly a much deeper issue for the girls.

During the course of this discussion, first the girls and then the boys gathered around us. Jane and Erin were the spokeswomen for the girls. This is especially significant because they were neither strong academic students nor leaders among the girls in the beginning of the year. Yet they were the ones most willing to take the risk to think about these issues and try to explain them. These girls were only in first grade, yet they had experienced bigotry, oppression, and discrimination. They were aware of it and they were able to find the words to discuss it. They knew it was inherently wrong and that it was hurtful; it hurt *them*. They stated that they couldn't help that they were female or that they liked girls things. Already, at this young age, they were unwilling to face rejection, and so conferred mostly with other girls. They were able to see this discrimination in a larger context, by comparing it to the issue of race. They were also realistic. Jane ended the discussion doubting that change was possible.

The Boys' Literacy Club

The boys' literacy club was the dominant feature of this classroom. Don didn't really belong, but he was tolerated. He was allowed to speculate on why the boys preferred not to confer with the girls. Rashi, on the other hand, was not allowed into the conversation. The last two lines of the first interview segment show that the boys are yelling at him for saying the same thing they have just shared. Rashi was forced to become an outsider, he wasn't even allowed to speak. At one point, Bart, the dominant leader in the group, told Rashi he had spoiled it all. Rashi immediately apologized.

The rules of the boys' literacy club were clear to the insiders, but obscure to the others. When Don tried to understand and explain the rules, he was tolerated, whereas Rashi was silenced. Rashi was the outsider, the only boy in the class who shared this status completely with the girls. The boys' literacy club was a hierarchy dominated by Bart, who invented many of the rules and granted status to the other boys, in part by how they followed the rules.

Although conferences had been modeled and shared in large and small group sessions, in mini-lessons, and in daily classroom life, Bart had reinvented the rules for the boys' literacy club. Bart's rules required the boys to sit together, write stories jointly, talk while writing, but not to participate in conferences. These rules were essentially secret, so that Bart could appear to endorse conferences while refusing to participate in them.

BART: Well, I never have a conference so I guess you could say no.

RH: But have you asked a girl to have a conference?

BART: Well, I never have a conference so I guess you could say no.

This negative view of conferences was reflected in the comments of other members of the boys' literacy club.

RH: How many times, let's say, did you conference today?

BART: Today neither, well I haven't conferenced once.

MARTY: I had a conference.

ALAN: Zero.

JERRY: I haven't conferenced, not even once.

Many times during the discussion, several boys would begin talking. If Bart was involved, he always established dominance, many times even interrupting me and continuing with his own agenda. By refusing to conference at all, Bart made it extremely difficult for outsiders to join the boys' literacy club. In fact, the unspoken rule of the boys' literacy club was that you had to be a boy, preferably a mainstream boy that Bart approved of. However, because the no conference rule was secret, the boys spent a lot of time justifying why girls were not suitable conference partners.

The toll of exclusion weighed heavily on Rashi and Don. Both boys found it difficult to fit in and had outbursts of disruptive and/or hostile behavior. Both were functioning below their potential in academics. Their rejection by the boys' literacy club negatively affected their behavior in the classroom. However, since membership in the boys' literacy club required one to be a Euro-American boy and not participate in conferences, there was little that outsiders could do to join this club.

Literacy provided the backdrop that allowed Jane's and Erin's insights to be articulated. As members of a collaborative, interpretive literacy community, they had found that their voices were valued and sought after. Each day they experienced many invitations and demonstrations (Cambourne 1989). The writing workshop provided a safe, predictable place where students were supported in their risk-taking. Students experienced ample opportunities for literacy immersion, approximation, and feedback. Because thinking and storytelling were valued, students saw themselves as co-constructors of meaning (Wells 1992). Because exploratory talk (Barnes 1976) was honored in the classroom, Erin and Jane were able to think about and discuss difficult issues for a prolonged period of time, in spite of their lack of experience and vocabulary.

Without these factors, Jane and Erin's voices wouldn't have been heard. They supported each other as they struggled to articulate their experience as girls. Often Erin would hesitate, Jane would attempt to describe, and then Erin would support Jane's attempts to articulate their experience. But this was a difficult feat. They were the only two girls who successfully described their experience. More accomplished girls in the class stood silent, shaking their heads but speaking little. Perhaps it was the experience of talking to the researcher each week that made the difference. Perhaps Jane and Erin got so used to metacognitively examining their thoughts and decisions that they were able to articulate an otherwise deeply inarticulate experience for girls and women even much older than they are.

Rashi was not so lucky. Because he was as an outsider, few wanted to collaborate with him. His behavior grew more outrageous, leading to reprimands and further isolation. The boy who began first grade with enthusiasm and excitement grew angry and distracted. Though he began first grade already reading, by the end he had withdrawn from books and writing.

Conclusions

It was particularly disturbing for me to realize how much I hadn't seen as I participated in the classroom community. I had assumed that Sadkers' (1994) studies and Orenstein's book (1994) had little to do with my own work. I didn't begin this research expecting to study gender and equity issues, and it wasn't easy for me to see as I taught in the classroom. For a long time, I didn't realize that the girls were almost exclusively conferring with each other, even though I spent time with them every week. I didn't see

Bart dominating the boys, yet it occurred in front of me. Rashi's pain was also invisible to me.

I still believe that the writing workshop serves an important literacy function in the classroom. The discrimination and inequities were wider than the classroom and reflected society at large. I now believe that, as teachers, we must help our students to examine social injustice and take action (Edelsky 1994). For children to grow up and create a more democratic world, we must insure that they experience democracy in our classrooms. Students need to talk about injustices and change them.

Whatever the reason, discrimination among students in elementary classrooms merits a closer look. How can we foster classrooms in which all children are equal, before we truly understand the classroom culture? The socialization of both boys and girls enters the first–grade classroom. These classrooms need to be examined carefully through multiple lenses. The issues of gender, race, ethnicity, social class, and other factors that lead to oppression need to be reported. Who is being included and who excluded in our classrooms? How does this affect the self-concepts and literacy development of those excluded students? And what real changes can we promote in both our classroom communities and the communities of the world to insure that real, deeper change may one day be possible? These questions have guided my work and led to this book.

2 | What Do We Mean When We Say Diversity?

What's in a word? Plenty. Words define us and date us. Words force us to be specific and say what we mean. In our effort to be as fair as possible, and because language is always changing, our quest for the most accurate word is never over. For a while, we used the word *minority* when referring to women and people of color. This word was actually a misnomer, for this group constitutes the majority of people living on this planet.

In searching for a better description, the term *people of color* began to be used. More and more however, the specific group is cited. For example, instead of saying *Latino*, we'd say *Mexican-American*. Another term that reflects this soul-searching is *historically oppressed groups*. This could be seen as a lens describing more than race, widening to include those who have also suffered injustice because of religion, culture, sex, and gender identification.

Multicultural Education

The term, *multicultural* has been used widely. This word has been criticized because it can mean so many things to so many people, but the definition that Sonia Nieto uses in her book, *Affirming Diversity* is one that I affirm:

> **Multicultural education:** A process of comprehensive and basic education for all students. Multicultural education challenges and rejects racism

and other forms of discrimination in schools and society and accepts and affirms the pluralism (ethnic, racial, linguistic, religious, economic, gender, etc.) that students, their communities, and teachers represent. They represent it and it is honored and respected in their classrooms. Multicultural education permeates the curriculum and instructional strategies used in schools, as well as the interactions among teachers, students and parents, and the very way that schools conceptualize the nature of teaching and learning. Because it uses critical pedagogy as its underlying philosophy and focuses on knowledge, reflection, and action (praxis) as the basis for social change, multicultural education furthers the democratic principles of social justice. Social justice is the responsibility you embrace and take on as a teacher. When such a thing happens, it reflects one of the tenents of democracy. Classroom communities of people no longer have to deal with prejudice and oppression, and children have the opportunity to express their identity openly.

Factors in Oppression

When used this way; the terms *multicultural education* and *historically oppressed* bring us closer to one of the ideas that Iris Young talks about in her book, *Justice and the Politics of Difference*. She talks about the idea of the cultural superiority of the dominant group in power, which promotes the dominant group as "normal" and renders other groups invisible. Iris Young has identified five factors of oppression that discriminated groups often face: ". . . exploitation, marginalization, powerlessness, cultural imperialism, and violence . . ." (p. 64). Although these terms are generally understood, the term cultural imperialism needs more explanation. Iris Young says that cultural imperialism applies to the kinds of oppression that exploit, marginalize, and oppress people who are not in power. She says that we need to look at who benefits from keeping things the way they are and who doesn't (p. 58). Young goes on to explain that since the dominant group controls the culture, those without power are marked as outsiders. "They are both marked out by stereotypes and at the same time rendered invisible" (p. 59). She adds that these groups are often seen as deviant and inferior.

The five factors (exploitation, marginalization, powerlessness, cultural imperialism, and violence) become useful in discussions of historically oppressed groups. It allows us multiple ways to talk about oppression. Rather than argue about which group has faced more oppression, Young suggests that if a group of people has faced any of these factors, it has suffered oppression, and that we need to work together to counter injustice wherever we find it.

I especially like this concept of multiple factors because each group has a different history of problems, and the factors begin to give us a language in which we can explore both our differences and our commonalities.

For instance, people of color have faced all five factors of oppression, as have women. Historically, all five factors have affected the Jewish people, while even today Jews suffer cultural imperialism and violence. Young suggests that if any one of these oppressions are present, the group is discriminated against. This helps us to include more groups that we may have overlooked before. Lesbians and gay men are not mentioned in Sonia Nieto's definition of multicultural education, except as an afterthought. This invisibility plagues lesbians and gay men, allowing society to ignore them in their multiple roles as partners and co-parents. They suffer violence and cultural imperialism; they suffer injustice in America. So do the children growing up in these families and sitting in classrooms across the country.

People in historically oppressed groups don't want to lose their identity in the mainstream. The pride of each group can be seen through the insistence of using the term *Puerto Rican* rather than *Latino* whenever possible. But all groups facing discrimination share in the desire to end the oppression they face. The challenge for schools and for society is teaching children to respect each group while ending the injustices perpetuated against them.

I decided to use "equity and social justice" in my title as a way of expressing this idea. It's not enough for children to know that discrimination and oppression are wrong; we must help them find ways to combat it. This book is about creating more equitable classrooms. In an effort to include children who feel othered for any number of reasons, I'm trying to widen the net. Although I'm talking about many oppressed groups in the course of the book, I'm not able to speak about many groups in detail. There are wonderful books that describe individual groups. My focus will be on diversity as a whole and, at the same time, a few of the individual groups as appropriate. I do not mean to slight a group or to imply that one group suffers more than another. "Building classrooms for diversity." What does this really mean? We need to affirm each child's identity and heritage. That's where we begin.

3 | Why Is Diversity so Difficult?

No one would argue against diversity and multiculturalism. We all want our children to get along with many different kinds of people. We want our children and our students to be able to think about complicated issues and see many points of view. The problem arises when we try to live within our belief systems. Even though we *say* that we embrace complexity, we still yearn for simple solutions.

Multiculturalism, diversity, and gender equity are widely discussed in education today. We talk about wanting diverse classrooms where all children can succeed, be heard, and form friendships with each other. Is this realistic? Is it possible to have multicultural, equitable classrooms in today's complicated world?

As educators we believe that if only we can do enough, help enough, facilitate enough, all our students will embrace literacy and learn. Discrimination and recriminations will leave our classrooms, and harmony will prevail. We believe that if we concentrate on a problem, we can fix it. And if we can't, it's because we haven't come up with the answers yet, but we will.

Start with Ourselves

There have always been outsiders in schools. These students have been dismissed by others, even by their teachers. These are the children who are different in some way. They walk a bit awkwardly, or their skin is the "wrong color," or they have a different religious or ethnic background, or they are overweight, or they don't dress like the others, and so forth. How do we begin to include the outsiders? We start with ourselves.

I've spent most of my life in hiding. My first, most conscious hiding was as a Jew. Even though my parents worked hard to make me feel proud, I still felt the sting of being an outsider at an early age.

My parents moved us to Skokie, Illinois when I was four years old. At the time, Skokie had one of the largest populations of Jews in the United States. I went to school with many other Jewish children. But my parents could not protect me from the world, try as they might. The particular block I lived on was mostly Christian. I remember spending Christmas mornings pressing my nose to the windowpane and wondering why Santa always stopped at my friends' houses, but never mine. It didn't matter what my parents said or their explanations about why Jews didn't celebrate Christmas. I wanted to celebrate Christmas. Wasn't I a good girl? I thought Santa went to all of the good children's homes. What had I done wrong?

I couldn't understand later on why the kids from St. Joan of Arc school were chasing me on their bikes. I was running through Central Park trying to get away from them. They were screaming, "Jesus killer, Jesus killer." I ran from them as if my life depended on it. Maybe it did.

How do we talk about the inequities of classroom life without confronting our own personal histories and admitting both the pain we felt as children, and the pain we continue to feel as adults? Before I can be a more sensitive teacher, I have to be able to confront the prejudices I've experienced in my life. I need to come to the classroom fully conscious and fully alive.

Writing Our Own Life Stories

I believe that literacy offers us powerful avenues in which to explore stories, both our students' and our own. Writing and telling our stories is the first place where we can begin to explore social justice. Reading about other peoples' lives allows us an insider's view into cultures and peoples, and extends our insights beyond ourselves.

The power of the narrative has been demonstrated over the centuries, and has been highlighted in education over the last decade. We use stories as a lens for research and we highlight stories in writing workshops. Certainly, long-term journal keepers and diary keepers have intuitively known the power of recording the stories of their lives.

I've kept a journal/diary since fifth grade. Most of the volumes sit in the black trunk my parents bought me when I went away to college. I wrote when the need arose—which was often—as a child, teenager, and young adult. I wrote because I had to. Often there was a pressing problem. Until I had committed my thoughts to paper, I wasn't able to make sense of my emotions and thoughts. I often felt a catharsis when I finished writing.

The journal wasn't a place that I would revisit very often. Although occasionally I might reread a section, I didn't dwell on the past. I solved major problems in my life, or thought about issues in as many ways as possible. When the problem was resolved, I had no need to look back.

Portfolios

However, when we use our life stories as a springboard for understanding others, we must be reflective. It's not enough to say "This is what happened." We have to try to understand what it means. Portfolios provide one way to help with this process. In a sense, portfolios tell our life stories, or at least a partial, educational story. But the core of the portfolio is the learner's reflections contained within. Without the reflections, the portfolio's potential is untapped.

This reflective element is especially important if we want our classrooms to become truly safe for all of our students. To have classrooms where everyone feels safe and no one is silenced is difficult indeed. It calls for a democratic and equitable society, one that many of our students may never have experienced in their lives. How do we create a life that some of our students cannot envision? We start with our stories and we reflect on their meanings.

Understanding the Experiences of Others

What do we know about the outsiders' experience in our classroom anyway? What do we know about the experience of the historically marginalized? Except for our own minority experiences, how can we imagine the lives of our marginalized students? Even with the best of intentions, what harm do we do in our ignorance?

In schools, we deal with real conditions that may be out of our control. However, it does help to think about some of these issues in a deeper way. We think that we understand complicated ideas like diversity and multicultural issues. We understand, at least in theory, that we have to be prepared to live with complexity and ambiguity. But how many times when faced with difficult decisions do we try to simplify things? We yearn for the one right answer, even when we understand cognitively that it is impossible.

For instance, my nephew Sasha attended La Honda Elementary School in La Honda, California since Kindergarten. It is a small, rural elementary school nestled in the mountains, near the ocean about half an hour south of San Francisco. We had always been impressed with the positive atmosphere, school community, and small class size that was made possible in part by the La Honda Foundation, where parents raised money for an additional teacher. Sasha and his parents were very happy there.

However, in the fall of sixth grade, over half of Sasha's class elected to attend the middle school in nearby Half Moon Bay. This meant that the remaining ten sixth–graders were divided up and put into the fifth and sixth or sixth and seventh multi-age classes. Neither of these situations was optimal, so Sasha decided to attend the middle school's orientation meeting.

Sasha was enthusiastic about the new school, but unsure. The family agonized about his placement and finally decided to transfer him to the middle school. The decision had to be made quickly. Still not sure about the choice, Sasha started middle school in Half Moon Bay.

The first day was a disaster. Sasha left a small, friendly elementary school for a huge middle school. He knew few students and was left alone most of the day. Only one of his friends from La Honda moved to the new school with him. He had no one to sit with at lunch, which seemed to go on forever. His physical education class was the worst. The teacher yelled at the boys the whole time because they couldn't open their gym locks. This was the first time any of the children had locks, and they all needed practice in opening them.

Sasha came home after the first day in tears. He hated the school and wanted to go back to La Honda. Even though his parents knew there would be an adjustment period, it broke their hearts to see him in so much pain. "I don't know if I should have done this," my sister confided to me on the phone the next morning. "Why aren't there any easy answers? It's not right."

I find that I, too, want easy answers. I might profess to be open to multiple possibilities, but it all breaks down the minute I'm confronted with contrary opinions. When my daughter was getting married, her fiancé decided that he didn't want any children at his wedding reception. I was brokenhearted that the three children I was closest to weren't going to be able to attend this momentous family event. Family members were irate, and threatened not to come. When some didn't, I felt under extreme duress. I couldn't believe my future son-in-law didn't understand the complications caused by his decision. I wanted everyone to interpret the situation in the way I did and to see that there was only one option, the solution that I wanted.

It didn't happen that way. Children were not invited to the reception. It turns out that I had to live with a complex, ambiguous situation that caused me and those I love pain. To me, this incident points out so clearly the difference between intellect and emotions. For although theoretically I was prepared to accept diversity and multiple perspectives, I found it much harder to live the reality.

The term *multicultural* is also given much attention, but while teachers express their understanding of multicultural awareness, living with this philosophy is considerably harder. There is still a need for the right answer that defies the reality of living in a complex world. Multiple interpretations and realities are hard to affirm in the classroom as well as in personal life. Complexity may describe our world, but human beings have difficulty living with conflicting values and multiple traditions. While this is a challenge for all people, it becomes critical for teachers to examine and deal with these issues if they hope to provide meaningful literacy experiences and authentic audiences for their children.

How well do you really know the students in your classroom? How do you know that the invitations and assignments in your classroom don't unintentionally bring pain to one of your students or to your students' parents? There are all kinds of families, and the one thing they have in common is that most of them could use more support. Not many people acknowledge good parenting. There are intact families that face some or extreme distress. Do you really understand the financial problems of some of your students' families?

Step-families may be flourishing, but still need support. The family tree assignment that is given out several times over a school career can cause pain to the non-biological family member(s). How about an assignment that celebrates the child's family? Why not add additional lines for all the parents and their families? This acknowledges the non-biological parents in a supportive way.

Perhaps gay and lesbian families present the greatest problems. Often, because we don't know what to say or how to act, we end up ignoring them. Regardless of how we feel about lesbian and gay families, we need to support the families, because our students are living in them. No, not in your classroom? Think again. Homosexuals make up at least 10% of the population, and many of them live in family units with children. Besides the previously married spouses who bring children with them into the new family, lesbians and gay men are also adopting and choosing to get pregnant and raise children together. It is unlikely that during your school career you won't ever have children from these families.

Often, gay and lesbian families are strong and have many positive things going for them. The children in these families are very wanted, with parents going to great extremes to conceive and adopt them. Even the most stable family has worried about custody battles, and the commitment to raising these children is very strong. However, every time we acknowledge only one parent (usually the biological one) and ignore the other, we do damage to the family. We're saying that the only parent who counts is the biological one. Even though the non-biological parent may love the child just as much, is at home with the child for longer periods, or is actually more involved in the child's homework, our actions are saying that this second parent doesn't count.

We may not mean for this to happen, but when we ignore family members, we render them invisible. We diminish their contributions to the family and we undermine our students' best chance for support and help in school. We didn't mean anything, we just didn't know how to act. Unfortunately, as teachers we no longer have that luxury. We have to use every means available to support our students' families, in order to insure our students' best chances for learning.

4

The Worst Thing You Can Call a Boy Is a Girl

My second grandchild was due in the middle of December. Since my son Ron and daughter-in-law Melody were living in Watertown, New York while we lived in Chicago, we drove up a week before the baby was due. Early in the morning, five days later, Ron took Melody to the hospital while we were left to babysit three-year-old, Ronny. Faced with the prospect of entertaining this very active boy for the entire day, we decided to take him to the mall.

Ronny was ecstatic. He ran up and down the walkways with two frantic grandparents struggling to keep up with him. He ran out of sight and we panicked. Finally we saw him playing with a truck in a toy store. I grabbed his hand and suggested that we look at other toys. As we walked through the aisle filled with dolls, Ronny said, "Girls' toys. Not for boys. Yuck!"

I was stunned. How could such a young child make this distinction? I had already thought about buying him a baby doll so that he had his own baby to take care of when his brother came home, but Ronny wanted no part of this.

My sister and brother-in-law live in La Honda, California. They are the older parents of pre-teen Sasha. They've worked hard to create a non-sexist home. Rudy and Sue both volunteer in the classroom. Rudy cooks meals more often than Sue does. Both of them value reading and writing and read and to him every night. However, when Sasha visited his grandparents a few years ago, he took my father aside and said, "Boys are really better than girls, aren't they Grandpa?"

A famous educator was in town for a conference. We were having dinner and a reception for him at my house, about half an hour from the conference site. He sat next to me as I drove. Lissa, one of my graduate students, sat quietly in the back seat and listened as I tried starting a conversation with him.

"So, are you happy here?" I asked.

"Oh, yes. While I miss my native country, I enjoy living in the U.S."

"Would you go back home if you had the chance?"

"I would, but that's unlikely. There aren't many university jobs over there."

"Would your wife go with you?" I asked politely.

"Now that's an interesting question," he responded. "You know, she's not my first wife. I'm not sure if she'd accompany me or not. After all, wives come and go."

Before I had time to react, he initiated another topic.

"I don't approve of all this feminist stuff you do," he said.

"What?" I asked in disbelief, thinking that I must have misunderstood him.

"Worrying about girls talking. Telling teachers to give girls a chance. It's ridiculous. It's a boys' world. All you're really doing is making boys conform to your idealistic vision of how the world should be. The world isn't fair. It's a man's world, and you're preventing boys from living in it. Boys get more opportunities, and there's nothing you can do. You're taking away boys' chances to practice their roles."

In her autobiography, Margarethe Cammermeyer (1995) talks of her subservient position in her Norwegian-American family: "My father tells everyone that he has four children. My four brothers are incensed every time he says this. Because I am female, I'm not worth counting."

When my sister graduated from college with her degree in business, our beloved Uncle Harry took her aside and bestowed his sage advice upon her: "Don't get your hopes up," he counseled. "You might get hired, but you'll never rise to the top. I don't care what anyone says. It's still a man's world."

Perhaps, individually, these stories could be dismissed as isolated incidents. However, it's more common than might be imagined. Each time I share my research with female educators, the stories emerge:

"College was out of the question in my family," recalls Esther Siva. "I was only a girl. I had saved money and thought that if I lived at home, I could manage. My mother outright refused. She said it was a waste of time to educate a girl."

"In high school, my calculus teacher called me aside. He told me that even though I had received the highest grade on every test, he was giving me a C for my final grade because there were no careers for girls in math." Mary Lou Daughterty recounts this story, which even today is painful for her. "He told me that he was doing me a favor, and that I'd thank him someday. I walked out of the class and never went back. That was the last math class of my life. The joke is I've spent my career working in banking and with computers. I use math, everyday."

Many young women today tell me that they have no need for feminism, that they are already equal and that they face no discrimination. When I talk about outsiders in the classroom, teachers of both sexes and of all ages tell me that they have no outsiders, that in their classes, everyone gets along. These teachers are sure. They know their students. It's just not a problem for them. Except that it is. When they begin looking, they suddenly begin to see.

Liz Desmond, a second-grade teacher in a suburb of Chicago asks, "How come the only parents who complain there isn't enough competition in my class are parents of the boys?" Claudia was one of the high school students featured in the 1996 NCTE/WLU video-conference, *What Matters*. As we watched the video of her class' literature discussion, we noticed that several of the boys dominated the conversation. When Claudia was asked about this, she explains:

> "It wasn't exactly random. . . . The teachers didn't exactly look for students who had special speech talents and who were gifted at talking or anything. There was Marianne, and she didn't say a word, but . . . she still got a lot from what she was listening to. . . .
>
> . . . The other thing that I wanted to talk about was everybody's been asking me, "Oh, did you feel the guys really wanted to dominate the group and everything?" That really didn't happen. It wasn't an issue for us. . . . We didn't check if we were wearing a skirt or pants when we decided to talk. We just wanted to talk and get out there. And if it just happened to be Doug, Dan, or Darrell, which it almost always was, it really didn't affect the rest of the group."

So even though the boys dominated the discussion almost exclusively, Claudia assures us that it isn't a problem. Except that it is a problem. As a society, we're so used to gender discrimination, we don't even notice it. We're so used to inequities that it's the equitable behavior that makes us feel uncomfortable!

What do we do in our classrooms when half the class isn't invited to share simply because they are female? How does this interfere with our community building? How can we use literacy to build both community and equity?

"Women still aren't always treated seriously in schools," says Graydon Love, principal of Woodlawn Hills Elementary School in San Antonio. "When I try to understand the inequities, I think about my own family history." Mr. Love is interested in genealogy and has been researching his ancestors. "Did you know that women in Virginia couldn't own land?" he asks. "Neither could they buy or inherit land in the recent past. No wonder there is so much more work to do."

The culture of the school duplicates the culture of the world. I was teaching a graduate class in the school's library. Lu Ann Stokes, one of the teachers in this class, looked around at the library books as we were discussing this issue. She focused her attention on the biography section. Of the fifteen books prominently displayed on top of the shelves, thirteen were about men, while only two were about women.

"Haven't you ever noticed," asks teacher Terri Poole, "that we don't have a single national holiday that honors women? We were talking about that in my teacher's lounge. What kind of message does that give to children?"

There are so many ways that we reinforce cultural stereotypes. Every time we ask the boys and/or the girls to line up, their differences are highlighted. "You know what's really funny?" asks Kindergarten teacher Marie Barkowitz. "If I call the boy's line, they all start yelling and making fists and getting excited. When I call the girl's line, they just quietly get up."

"How come the boys are so much more aggressive?" we wonder. "Are they used to getting more attention? Do we as teachers naturally give them more attention without even noticing? Or do we reinforce certain behaviors that cause boys to act out and girls to remain quiet?"

I think of my son Ron, and the way he is raising his sons to fight and act out. Their favorite television show is "Wrestling Mania." The boys take turns throwing their wrestling toys on the floor and jumping all over them. They yell and shout and run wildly around the house. When asked how he

Will of James Hays, Senior of Albemarle County, Va.

I, James Hays Senior, of Albemarle County, being of sound mind and memory, do make this my last will and testament, thereby revoking all others that I have made. First it is my will that all my just debts be paid and that my Executor sell as soon as possible after my death my tract of land lying in Augusta County adjoining the town of Wainsborough also my land in Augusta County called Mathasiass tract which I purchased in partnership with Jacob Kenney also my land lying part in Nelson County and part in Albemarle and part in Augusta which I purchased in partnership with James Brooks of Frances Hogg be sold and the money arising from the sales the land be applied to the payment of my just debts also the tract of land I purchased of James Roberson in Albemarle be sold and the money applied to just debts also my personal estate be sold and the money applied to the payment of my just debts and the balance after paying my debts be equally divided between my nine children to wit: James, David, Issac, Nathaniel, Thomas, William, Mary, Sarah, Malinda; and my will is that the tract of land I now live on including the land I bought of Valentine Shutts containing about one thousand acres be the same more or less be equally divided between my three sons to wit James, Nathanial and Thomas. My said three sons is to pay my three daughters five hundred pounds each after they arrive at the age of twenty one years to wit James to pay Mary five hundred pounds after she arrives at the age of twenty one at the rate of two hundred dollars a year until the said five hundred pounds is paid and his part of the land liable to be sold to pay the said sum of five hundred pounds to Mary, my daughter. Also Nathaniel to pay Sarah Ann five hundred in the same way after she arrives at the age of twenty-one years James is to pay Mary and his part liable to be sold in the same way as James part is also liable Thomas is to pay my daughter Malinda five hundred pounds in the same way as James and Nathaniel is to pay Mary and Sarah Ann after she Malinda arrives at the age of twenty one years and his part liable to be sold in case he fails to pay the said sum of five hundred pounds to my said daughter Malinda Hays; my will is that the boys parts of my land mentioned above liable to be sold to pay my daughters their legacies is not to be sold until the last payment becomes due; my will is that my said three daughters live with my son James until they arrive at lawful age or until they should marry and my will is that my Executor school my said daughters as much as they think is common for them to have and see that they have sufficient maintenance until they arrive at the age of twenty one or until they may marry and the expenses of Education and Maintenance to be paid out of their legacies before mentioned. My will is that my son James take immediate possession of the house I now live in at my death and my will is that my son William pay my Executors one hundred pounds before he receives any part of my Estate which sum I have paid for him some time ago and that my Executors pay one hundred dollars to Claudius Buster out of Williams' part provided they may have as much in their hands which said Buster paid for my son William some time ago. My will is that my executors pay unto Claudius Buster fifty pounds after paying my other debts and one horse saddle and bridle to be valued at not less than eighty no more that one hundred dollars the said fifty pounds and horse saddle and bridle is left to him for his kind treatment to me and not for anything I owe him. I have not mentioned my son John Hays nor my daughter Elizabeth married to Robert Brooks but I would wish it understood I have not forgot them by not mentioning them as I have given them their legacies some time ago and lastly I appoint my friends Jechoviaz Yancey my son James Hays and Thomas Martin Executors of this my last will and testament. In witness whereof I have hereunto set my hand and seal this 16th day of December One thousand eight hundred and twelve.

Copy of will of Graydon Love's great-grandparent.

and his wife can stand it, Ron shrugs his shoulders. " What can I do?" he says. "You know, boys will always be boys. It's not as if I have anything to do with it."

Teaching elementary school during the 1970s, I had high hopes for my students. I encouraged the girls to enjoy the same activities as the boys. I urged them to wear sensible clothes, perhaps jeans, a t-shirt, and gym shoes to school so that they were free to move around and get dirty. I nudged them to play games with the boys during recess, and to participate in basketball, soccer, and baseball. But my invitations were rarely successful. Only one girl, Jeri, really participated in the physical games. Most of my female students watched from the sidelines. Twenty-five years later, although we've made some progress, not a lot has changed. But it can.

We can make sure that our classroom and school libraries carry many books with strong female characters and males in non-traditional roles. Girls and women can be well-represented in every genre. We can display biographies that are equally distributed between men and women's contributions. On holidays, we can encourage students to research and share women's achievements, creating women's holidays, too. Using literacy, we can share the stories of both sexes' achievements.

5 | Talk, Diversity, and Gender: Trying to Communicate

A curious thing happens when you start noticing gender inequities. Suddenly you can't stop seeing them. You notice them in the classroom and at home. In every social situation you become aware of the different ways that males and females seem to inhabit their worlds. You want to make a difference. You want to help boys and girls communicate better. So what do you do? Those of us who have been entrusted with the education of children have this incredible opportunity to influence the future. How do we know we are doing the right thing?

Dr. Deborah Tannen is a socio-linguist who has written many books and articles for both academic and general readers in an effort to shed some light on the situation. Her best–known book is *You Just Don't Understand* (1990), in which she discusses the communication problems that men and women run into, not because they're angry with each other but because the genders communicate differently. Tannen has found that whereas men's conversation might focus on solving problems, women talk to show affiliation. Whereas men may concentrate on status, women's talk focuses on building community. So when men and women try to communicate, they became get frustrated by each other's style of communication.

Tannen illustrates her point with a couple who is trying to decide where they would like to go for dinner. The conversation begins:

MAN: "Where would you like to eat tonight?"

WOMAN: "I don't know, anywhere. You decide."

This might sound like an agreeable conversation, but this couple is on the road to conflict. The man wants a resolution quickly, so they can go out for their meal. The woman wants to bond through the conversation, compromising if necessary. She wants to give him an opportunity to express his preference. But the conversation goes downhill from here. The man grows irritated with the woman because she doesn't make a choice; the woman gets upset with the man when he ultimately chooses a restaurant that she doesn't like.

What happens in an exchange like this? Communication styles cause conflict. The couple wasn't angry with each other when they began the conversation, but they were by the time it ended. The man wanted to solve the problem (where to eat) as quickly and efficiently as possible. The woman wanted to talk for awhile, and make the decision together.

Deborah Tannen goes on to explain that cultural styles also influence the way we talk. For instance, people living in the East, as well as Jewish Americans, tend to talk quickly, enjoy arguing, and have very fast-paced conversations. Speakers interrupt each other to show understanding. Tannen calls this phenomenon *high-involvement talk*. Speakers from the West Coast and the South tend to talk more slowly. Interruption is viewed as rude. Tannen describes this as the *high-politeness communication style*. Neither is right or wrong, but depending on the situation, speakers of either communication style could find themselves in conflict.

A Thanksgiving Day meal was the subject of Dr. Tannen's dissertation. Gathered around the table were friends from the East Coast and West Coast, and one person from England. Three of the participants were New York Jews of Eastern European background. They were the most involved in the discussion, interrupting each other most often, and therefore sharing the floor. All three enjoyed the discussion very much. The fourth person was a New York Italian. He, too, was used to the high-involvement conversational style and enjoyed the evening. The fourth participant who had 386 conversational turns was from Berkeley and at home with fast-paced conversations.

The other three participants reported that they felt left out. No one really cared about their opinions or they would have been let into the conversation. They felt the talkers were rude. Two of these participants were from California and used to a relaxed, slower conversational style. One of these was deaf, but the second interpreted for him. These three expected pauses where other participants could gain the floor. The third participant was Jewish, but from England where this high politeness style is even more evident.

Here's an example where cultural styles got in the way. Members from the high politeness conversational style had trouble entering the discussion. The other participants were happily talking, having no idea that they were leaving out the others. Implicit in the high involvement style is jumping in whenever you want to and joining in. Interruption is seen as affiliation. If people choose not to jump in, it's not because they are unhappy, but because they are satisfied listening. Once again, here's an example of people miscommunicating, not because they didn't like each other, but because they didn't understand each other's cultural communication styles. This may have resulted in not liking each other, but it didn't start out that way. One last point: Notice that Suzy, the Jewish woman from London, had much more in common with the West Coast conversational style than with the three Jews from New York. In the same way, the New York Italian Catholic had a lot in common with the New York Jews. In this case, the regional style was the overriding common conversational feature, rather than religion.

Linguists have found that linguistic features of the original language spoken by an immigrant group of people stays with the group long after they have several generations of native speakers in the adopted country. In a series of studies, Tannen found that native Greek speakers talk indirectly and value a good story over accuracy of details. When she studied Greek-Americans who spoke only English, she found these two characteristics present among their talk, too. So, although the language has changed, the characteristics of the original language remain with the speakers.

Once, I found myself in a situation where knowledge of someone's original way of speaking would have been helpful. My friend Adrienne's Greek family has been in the United States for generations, but sometimes we miscommunicate. Her long, fanciful stories are an enigma to me; she is often so indirect that I am confused by what she is trying to say. When my daughter Kathy graduated from college, she asked for a small party with a few friends. She wanted Adrienne to attend. When I called Adrienne to invite her to the party, Adrienne said, "Great! What would she like [as a gift]?" I replied that Kathy really needed something for her future apartment, and Adrienne suggested a big pot. I also noted that Kathy wanted a small party, with just a few friends. We agreed. At the end of the conversation, Adrienne remarked, "I don't want to get her something little; I want to get her something big, something respectable."

Several days later everything I had planned seemed to unravel. I discovered that Adrienne had phoned a number of our friends to see if they wanted to chip in with her for Kathy's gift; none of these friends had been invited to the party! I was mortified, but when I confronted Adrienne, she was not only defensive, she seemed to be reminding me that she had told me she was going to call all the friends. I couldn't remember this part of the conversation at all.

"When did you tell me this?" I asked.

"I told you I didn't want to give her something little," replied Adrienne. To Adrienne, my acknowledgment of her remark meant that I understood she would be calling friends to enlist their help. We ended up inviting the friends, and my friendship with Adrienne survived; but this incident stands as a reminder to me of the miscommunication that can result when cultural styles clash.

So now that I know about cultural styles, how can I do better next time? What's the first step? For me, the first step is knowing about it. I wish I had understood the variations in our cultural speaking styles much earlier in my friendship with Adrienne. I understand that not all Greek-Americans are indirect or would have reacted in this way. Adrienne is a unique individual. However, this information has helped me to understand her. I suspect that many instances of our miscommunication might have been cleared up earlier if only I had some insight into this. But Deborah Tannen warns us that just because you understand something about communication style doesn't mean that it will be easy to change.

I planned a doctoral students' meeting with one of my valued and trusted colleagues. I have always admired Mike's commitment to equality and fairness, and his brilliant mind as a scholar. Together we thought we would investigate the cultural styles of women and men, and then open the discussion to our doctoral students. We tried to decide the best format. Role-playing? Simulation? Video? Finally we decided to share a homemade video and then to role-play a discussion between the two of us. Role-play? Mike was enthusiastic, while I was unsure. It didn't seem authentic, and that bothered me. Mike wasn't worried about the issue of authenticity. He wanted to make sure it was provocative enough to make students uncomfortable and to think critically about the issues. Mike was the full professor, I was the new faculty member. Besides, since we both came from the same cultural background, we could be reasonably sure we were focusing on the differences between gender rather than cultural groups. I agreed to go along with his plan.

Our simulation was to begin as the teachers arrived. We planned to argue about how we would set up the room and how we would organize our activities for the evening. As soon as we began, though, I knew I couldn't go through with it. After we set up the tables in a circle so everyone could see each other, we spent fifteen minutes introducing ourselves and sharing why the topic has drawn us to this seminar. Then we explained that Mike and I were going to do a simulation, and we began.

I told Mike that I couldn't go through with our fake plan for a pretend conflict between us. It just felt too inauthentic to me. Besides, there were plenty of authentic things we could argue about. Perhaps the place to start was with the idea that we have to have controversy at any cost. Mike looked at me like he was stunned. He was silent, so I plunged ahead. Why would we have to fake anything? Didn't we trust that our interactions would provide enough data for a discussion to follow? Didn't we trust our students?

Mike recovered, and eloquently defended his position that discomfort can lead to new insights. We got into a lively debate that we both enjoyed, given our high-involvement communication styles. But I couldn't quite shake Mike's look at the moment he didn't speak. How could I change the discussion? This was something women don't do.

Our students noticed it too. Mike seemed shaken. Women aren't supposed to break the rules. He really believed his fake conflict was a good idea. He didn't see how inauthentic it felt to us. The graduate students noticed more about the interactions than Mike and I knew had taken place. Once they mentioned it, though, we could see there were many things going on in our interaction that were difficult for us to articulate. Later Mike would tell me that I had blind–sided him. He felt completely unprepared for my change of direction.

We showed the video next. My mother had taken this video in the home of one of my great aunts. My grandmother, who was then in her mid-nineties, is the oldest of five children. All but one of them is still alive. We had flown in for a family reunion. My mother, father, and I were visiting with my grandmother's two sisters and their spouses. When my great-aunts saw the video camera, they became animated and weren't sure what to do.

I told them that I felt honored to be in a room with so much accumulated wisdom and asked if they could share some of it with me. They were quiet for a while. "I'll tell you about my life," Uncle Harry began. He talked nonstop for what seemed like a long time. While he spoke, he had everyone's complete attention. After he finished, it was difficult for any of the sisters to get the floor. Finally Aunt Enid started to speak. "There's nothing interesting about my story," she said. "There never was anything special about me."

"What do you mean?" interrupted her husband, Uncle Harry. "Of course you were special. You were very beautiful. You had many boyfriends."

Aunt Enid conceded that maybe there had been a lot of boys following her around. My grandmother also felt that her story wasn't interesting. Nonetheless, she told us about her work at Marshall Field's & Company.

The gender dynamics in this family visit are quite interesting. Only the women were interrupted. Only the men felt comfortable having side conversations, getting up and walking around the room, and/or correcting the speaker. In all kinds of non-verbal ways, the message comes through: Men are more important than women. Uncle Harry begins the conversation because men go first. When Uncle Harry reprimands his wife, citing examples of her value, they all have to do with physical beauty and her desirability to men. Both my grandmother and her sisters accepted this behavior as the natural order of things.

It was interesting what my grandmother chose to talk about. She worked for only a few years after marrying my grandfather. She was a salesclerk at Marshall Fields & Company, at the department store's main site in downtown Chicago. She worked a relatively small amount of her adult married lifetime, but she has painted many pictures, which hang in all of our houses. I thought that she might have chosen to talk about her life as an artist, but she didn't. Even now, when she is forgetting so many things, she talks proudly of her days at Marshall Fields.

Once you become aware of gender inequities, your life is never the same. You see them everywhere you look. Once you are sensitized, it becomes impossible to ignore. But what do you do? Deborah Tannen warns us that dealing with gender styles isn't as easy as it looks. For instance, the same woman who looks weak when she doesn't confront a subordinate is seen as pushy when she does. Dr. Tannen describes one study of a group of new doctors. There was only one woman in a group of men. The veteran doctors and the new doctors all felt the female doctor was not as competent because she asked a lot of questions. The male doctors might not have known the answers either, but would probably not have admitted it. So asking questions made her seem less competent, because in the male model of communication it means weakness.

So, if the same female doctor were to stop asking questions would she be seen as more competent? Not necessarily. She could be viewed as arrogant simply for behaving like her colleagues. Even worse, the information she gained from asking questions helped to make her a better doctor; without asking them, she would lose access to that information.

So what do we do? That's a good question, and one that we're just starting to figure out. We begin by noticing and learning about gender and cultural styles. The more observant we are about previously unarticulated experiences, the better able we are to see what's happening. And the more we learn about and study gender and cultural communication styles, the better equipped we'll be to understand the interactions in our lives. Then we can begin to talk about what is happening with our students and help them to critique, too.

Perhaps, in the future, the following wouldn't have occurred. I was at a dissertation meeting with a doctoral student and two of my colleagues. The only male participant at the meeting, a colleague I respect and value, asked the student if gender issues was the only social issue she was interested in, because, to him, it seemed limited. He went on to say it was nice that she knew all about gender issues, but perhaps she should concentrate on something that was more difficult to understand, implying that gender inequity was a simple social problem. Clearly, our education is still beginning. And if it is a difficult issue in our lives, no wonder we have such difficulty in changing our classrooms. Equity in our classrooms is an important goal, one that requires all of our imagination, perception, and courage to achieve.

Even as we attempt to create gender equity in our classrooms, the world continues in a most inequitable fashion. Women in Kuwait have no legal rights. Men can divorce them at any time, but they can not initiate divorce themselves. They have no health benefits on their own, and, if divorced, must go home to their fathers or brothers, for they have to be under the protection of the males. Males have individual rights. Females don't. Women exist only as part of families.

Discrimination against women and other groups still exists in the United States and around the world today. *The Report on the World's Women 1995*, published by the United Nations, paints a grim picture of the violence that occurs against women around the world. "Gender-based violence

st women crosses all cultural, religious, and regional boundaries and is
ajor problem in every country in which it has been studied" (p.158).

The problem is that violence against women hasn't been studied nearly
enough. "In the United States, only a few women actually report rapes"
(p.158). This figure grows more oppressive when other issues are taken into
consideration. Violence against women occurs in every country in the
world. In most parts of the world, over 90 percent of the rape victims are
girls (and women), while over 90 percent of the perpetrators are men.
When questioned about why gender discrimination should matter to teachers, we need to point to these statistics. Discrimination against women and
girls leads to violence against women and girls. Education is the way to
change.

Promoting Equity in Classrooms

How do we create lasting change? How can we teach children to notice and
stand up against injustice? We can start with gender issues. There are specific things we can do as teachers to promote gender equity. These include:

• Not using the terms, "boys and girls" or "you guys" or "Mr. and Miss"
or "young men and young ladies." If you want the class to pay attention,
simply say, "class" or "fifth graders" or "students." We don't want to point
out to the children that they are different. Considering how many times
this can occur during a school day, teachers can be responsible for pointing
out differences between the sexes much more often that promoting similarities.

• Don't allow students to segregate themselves into single-gender
groups all the time. Have the students count off by numbers, or sit in groups
with equal gender distribution instead. You could have students' names on
index cards or popsicle sticks readily available. Then when it is time for
groups to form, you might quickly call the names on the sticks or cards in
random order.

• Make sure everyone is working together and that no one is ostracized.
Vivian Paley has written that in her class, "You can't say you can't play." In
Nancie Atwell's school in Maine, they take it even further. Children can't
say no to each other. If I ask to sit with you or conference with you or play
with you, you have to say okay. This is a school-wide rule and is applicable
at recess as it is in an individual class.

• In competitions or games, make sure each team has both boys and girls.
Don't allow boys and girls to compete against each other. Competitive games
like Spelling Bees serve to further divide the sexes if the teams are not mixed.

• Try to be conscious when calling on children to alternate between calling on boys and girls. Sadkur suggests using popsicle sticks or index cards with students' names on them as you're calling on students. This way, you know you're calling on everyone. Students always have the opportunity to pass if they don't want to speak.

• Establish a classroom where everyone gets a chance to speak. Once they have the floor, they keep it as long as they request it. This means longer than a minute if necessary, giving students a chance to pause to think. One way this might be accomplished is by passing out chips. Linda Christensen uses poker chips in her high school classroom in Portland, Oregon. She uses the colors to help ensure equity. When everyone with a red poker chip who wishes to speak has spoken, then students with black poker chips may cash them in by speaking. The black chips indicate the second round. Students must wait until everyone has had a chance in the first round. This way, no student can dominate with too many turns.

• Don't remind children that they are different sexes in school. Susan Crawford (1996) suggests the bias test when not sure of your practice. You could also call this the racist test, or the religious test, or the role reversal, or the test that gets at exclusion or invisibility or sexism. It works like this: If you're not sure if a behavior is sexist, reframe it. While saying "Good morning boys and girls," may seem harmless, would you ever say "Good Morning Blacks and Whites," or "Good Morning Jews & Christians?" If you wouldn't, don't use the original phrase. While these phrases may not be exactly the same, the point is to avoid pointing out differences to students.

• When forming lines, alternate between boys and girls. If the rest of your school uses separate lines of boys and girls, try to start a new trend. Mickey Nuccio says, "I've been thinking about this a lot. Why can't the kids simply step out of the line when it is their turn and go into the designated bathroom?" Perhaps you can develop a school policy where children don't have to go en masse to the washrooms, but instead allow individuals to go on an "as needed" basis.

• Model equity and fairness in the classroom. Set an example. Kids follow the teacher's lead. We want to make sure they know we're advocates for justice in our classrooms.

Using Literacy to Promote Gender Equity

Literacy can extend and expand our understanding of gender bias and the need for social justice in our classrooms. The following are some of the positive things we can do to promote gender equity in schools:

• Put the issues out front. Talk and reflect about them when conflicts and incidents occur in classrooms. Don't ignore injustice. If a student is picked on, don't ignore it. Make critical incidents the center of class discussions. Don't allow some students to dominate others. We know the power of discussion and problem-solving. Peer mediation and conflict-resolution programs in schools are growing more popular. Talk gives us a venue in which we can view the issues and reflect on them. It is critical that we use our intellectual powers to move toward equity rather than supporting the status quo.

• Choose books with strong females and pro-women visions for literature discussions. (There is a list of these books in the appendix.) Study women who have made contributions to the world. In the past, both men and women thought there had never been any great women writers or artists or scientists. In reality, there were many, but because the culture didn't value women, their accomplishments often went unnoticed. Now that we have an awareness of women's contributions to the culture, it is important to keep this information available. Without effort, the recent gains could be lost.

• Seek out books that have boys and men in non-traditional roles, working for peace. Remember the third–grade study that showed that the only boys who would consider non-traditional roles were those who saw men performing non-traditional tasks. Judith Solsken also cautions us about the need for children to see men reading and writing. Unfortunately, boys in her study came to view literacy as something that females do. They saw their mothers and teachers reading and writing, but rarely their fathers. It's not that these fathers didn't read, but they were more likely to read at work than at home.

Invite dads and grandfathers and as many males as possible to come and read with the kids. Ask them to talk about the non-traditional parts of their lives. Invite employees from local businesses such as banks and McDonalds to come and read to the students. Invite male and female sports coaches to read with the class.

• Study ads in the newspaper and offer inquiry units that include researching children's stores. Are there certain colors or other identifying characteristics of the boys' and girls' sections? For instance, why in the newspapers are the girls' sections pink and the boys' sections blue? Why, when you walk into so many toy stores, are the girls' aisles pink? What subtle messages come through? How does this affect the girls? How does this affect the boys? Does this segregation discourage boys from buying dolls and girls from buying trucks?

• Offer invitations for students to critique movies and cartoons. Do they believe that certain movies are for boys and others for girls? Why do some boys refuse to watch movies that star girls or have girls in the title? Why not watch *Pocahontas* or *Harriet the Spy?*

• Ensure that boys and girls confer together during writing workshop, work in small groups together, and write together. Don't leave it to choice. Give students some choice, but watch out for those who might be excluded.

• Validate the stories and interests of the girls as well as of the boys. Karen Evans found that in the classroom she was studying, the boys were reinforced by the teacher and the class for stories that the boys liked to hear but that most of the girls found wearisome. Sports stories and stories of violence were the boys' favorites. Sixth-grade teacher Faith Barbara-Mirza found that to be happening in her classroom as well. "Did I unconsciously promote those stories by my enthusiasm for them?" she wonders. The girls' stories, which focused more often on relationships, weren't supported in the same way.

• Study video games. Why do so many more boys like them, enjoy them, and play them? Why are the games designed, with a few exceptions, with boys in mind? (Why is one product called Game-Boy and not Game-Girl?)

• Encourage reflection and revision for students through author's theater. Students bring their first drafts to the author's theater, where the story is cast and students act out the parts. Encourage boys to play girl's parts and girls to play the boy's parts, explaining that this will give them a chance to experience things from a different point of view. This could even become one of the rules of author's theater.

• Encourage boys and girls to read about women who have made contributions to the world. Boys could be required to share what they've learned in their research. As they share their book or their research, they could speak as if they were the person. Girls could do the same thing, as well as having opportunities to speak as famous men.

• Study women as a class, especially women who've made significant contributions to the community. Peggy Nadziejko asked women from all walks of life to participate in her fifth–grade class project, *Women Who Make a Difference.* One woman worked for the Environmental Protection Agency, another was a hairdresser, and a third worked as a butterfly expert from the Butterfly House Shelter. Women dentists, doctors, and reporters were interviewed by students. A woman who worked at the local homeless shelter spent time with the students, and so did the mayor of the town, who is a woman. Students saw women in diverse work roles, and forged new friendships and mentors.

Crystal Vela

My Heroe

One of my heroes is Hilary Clinton. She is my heroe because she cares about the country. She goes around the world and gives speches about how to make the world a better place for future generations. She cares about Chicago and everything that will ever happen to Chicago. Hillary Clinton came to Chicago to give a speach and later on she went to the Bulls game and she was jest another fan.

Written
By
Crystal Vela

• Study sex role stereotypes from a critical perspective. Whose point of view is represented? Who wrote the script? Who benefits from the status quo? Who is hurt by the injustice? We've always encouraged students to ask questions and use the questions to guide their learning. Now we're nudging them even further. Even younger students can learn to look closer. Just because women weren't expected to hold jobs with responsibility didn't mean it didn't happen, wasn't possible, and isn't occurring now. Why did people think this? Who benefited from women not being allowed to hold responsible jobs? As students continually ask these questions, opportunities for discussion arise, which can create more opportunities for social justice to occur in the classroom.

• Pursue linguistic studies. For example, What is the origin of words like *mailman*? Why is the word *man* there? Is it meant to exclude women or is it meant to include both men and women? Why is the word man in *women*? Why is inclusive language important? What about words like *nagging, scolding,* or *henpecked*? (Crawford, 1996) How does this make girls and women feel? What about imbalanced word order like Mr. and Mrs.? How does the imbalance distort meaning? Who is selected as important? Why does a woman lose her last name when she marries, but not a man? Why does a woman lose even her first name if she is married and introduced formally, such as "Mr. and Mrs. John Snow?"

• Examine why the worst thing you can call a boy is a girl. What does this do to a girl's self-esteem? What does it do to boys who like girls? Why is it bad for boys to emulate girls, but fine for girls to emulate boys?

• Examine textbooks and novels for biased language and inaccurate and stereotyped gender images. Both teachers and students can check for this. Students could bring in examples of biased language from newspapers and magazines and comic books. Have them rewrite the examples more inclusively. Have them write letters to the publishers sharing their observations with recommendations for non- biased language use.

• Conduct inquiry projects on the playground. Students could investigate the words they overhear in conversations. In what context are they used? Are the words non-biased? This project could also be done at home. How do the words further inequities in treatment?

• Conduct inquiry projects on the playground that focus on play. Have students observe who is playing together during recess. What games are being played? For instance, who is playing football, baseball, or soccer? Are girls playing with the boys? How are the teams chosen? What is done to ensure that children don't suffer the shame of being the last one chosen? Are boys playing girls' games with the girls? This study could be done at home in the neighborhood, too.

• Tape discussions at home. Who talks the most? Who is talking the least? What words are used? Are some tasks during mealtime handled by one sex or the other? Why? How is this behavior useful? Who benefits? How could it be made more equitable?

• Encourage girls to pursue their interests across the curriculum, especially in math and science, and across the disciplines. Girls need to view all areas of the curriculum as interesting and potential areas in which they can make contributions and excel. Boys need to see girls in this way, too. Boys should also be able to pursue their interests in non-traditional areas of the curriculum, areas currently considered girls' territory without teasing, harassment, or loss of status.

• Teach students to speak out when they notice inequitable behavior and activities. Teachers need to speak out for justice, too. When unfair practices occur, they need to be changed. When biased language is used, it needs to be acknowledged and every effort needs to be made for change. When students find biased language and situations in their texts or in the newspapers or in the stores, they need to write letters and plan action. It's not enough just to know; you have to do something to fight injustice.

6

What If My Class Is Already Multicultural?

Social justice is important in all situations. Every group needs to learn about and respect others. Cross-cultural education helps us to see the universal in all peoples while at the same time affirming our own roots. Those of us who teach in situations where most of our children come from one background have even more of an obligation to teach social justice.

What if your class is homogeneous? First of all, that's unlikely. While it may not be as obvious, it's unlikely that every child in your classroom comes from the same cultural and social background. "In a way, it's easier if kids have similar backgrounds," says Kathy Feldheim, a first–grade teacher in the affluent suburb of Highland Park, Illinois. "We can talk about different cultural groups without making a child feel like an outsider."

This is an important point. Elizabeth Ellsworth (1989) found that her much older college students resented having to speak for their race or culture when issues came up. These articulate college students at the University of Wisconsin felt it was imperative that teachers educate themselves and not put them on the spot. So what can a well-meaning teacher do? Read, learn, go to cultural events, movies, exhibits, and join with others in inquiry. "Most importantly," says Kathy Feldheim, "we have to model for our students. We need to model inquiry. Our students have to see us accepting differentness and embracing diversity. They learn from us that there is nothing to be afraid of."

Teachers in Lorri Davis's graduate class decided that they needed to learn more about the African-American culture. After reading and discussing Lies *My Teacher Told Me: Everything Your American History Textbook Got Wrong*, by James Loewen, they planned a field trip to see Spike Lee's film about the Million Man March. After discussing the movie at the next class, they realized they needed more cross-cultural experiences, and so they planned a trip to the DuSable Museum of African American History to see the Underground Railroad exhibit.

Viewing the exhibit helped the teachers to understand the awful treatment African Americans have experienced in America. Many of the teachers were emotionally moved. They wrote in their journals and continued their joint inquiry, inviting an African-American teacher to share her experiences with them. They also created text-sets and had literature discussions using *Life on the Color Line. The True Story of a White Boy Who Discovered He Was Black* (Gregory Howard Williams) and *There Are No Children Here* (Alex Kotlowitz). Many of the teachers reported that they were changed forever by this experience.

This project illustrates the power of study groups and what can happen when teachers set out to educate themselves about injustice. We bring these experiences back into our classrooms and begin to change the structure of schooling.

How Does This Work if I Teach Thirty-five Hispanic Children?

This is critically important for our students and for society. The United States is becoming increasingly diverse. By 2020, one in every four children will be Hispanic, and 20 million children will be living in poverty, an increase of 37 percent (Au 1993, p. 3).

Bell Hooks (1994) calls for educators "to teach against the grain and to focus on multiculturalism in our society, particularly in education, there is not nearly enough practical discussion of ways classroom settings can be transformed so that the learning experience is inclusive" (p. 35). Literacy can become a vehicle for true multicultural teaching, and, conversely, this transformative teaching and learning community promotes literacy growth in our students.

The work of Luis Moll is particularly illuminating. Moll and his graduate students went into the working class homes of Hispanic students to develop reciprocal relationships and learn about the students' home lives. He found that the families knew a lot about many subject areas. Moll suggests that we use these families' "funds of knowledge" in our classrooms. This would help students make connections between home and school. Families funds of knowledge include:

"... cultivation of plants, folk remedies, herbal cures, midwifery, and first aid procedures, usually learned from older relatives. Family members with several years of formal schooling have knowledge about (and have worked in) archeology, biology, education, engineering, and mathematics. (Moll 1994, p.443)

Funds of knowledge, then, are the skills and knowledge of working–class and historically oppressed families. Moll believes in the transformative potential of these funds of knowledge for children in the classroom. He suggests that we invite parents into the classroom to share their expertise. This could lead to inquiry studies in the classroom. Moll is not suggesting that we invite parents in to talk about Martin Luther King and end the project there. Neither is he suggesting that a culture day when families bring in a dish from their culture will transform a classroom. For funds of knowledge to have transformative potential, parents have to be equal partners in the process.

Treat Students Like Neighbors

Moll suggests keeping in mind that parents may not be comfortable in the classroom at first. He suggests that a reciprocal relationship would be more like ones we have with friends, families, and neighbors. Establish an "I'll help you and you'll help me" relationship. These relationships work be-cause all the participants are equal and have something to share. For exam-ple, two little boys live next to me. David is in first grade and his brother Matthew is a third–grader. I know David and Matthew from our many neighborly chats. One Sunday last fall I took a walk around the neighbor-hood, and, while doing so, lost my house key. When I rang my neighbors' doorbell, Chuck, the boys' father; said he could help me get into the house. While he was doing so, I asked him how the boys were doing, and he replied that while Matthew was doing fine, David was having trouble in school. Chuck said that he and his wife Nanette were upset and not sure what to do. I told him that I was a reading teacher, and offered to work with David. He expressed concern that they couldn't pay me, and I told him not to worry about it.

"There must be something I could do," he said.

"You could fix the part of the fence that's falling down."

This began our friendship with our neighbors. It's been mutually beneficial for both households. When Nanette broke her leg, we watched the kids while she went to the hospital. David in particular was distraught, but allowed me to comfort him, something that he never would have done before I started tutoring him. When we were out of town for a prolonged period of time, the Todds and their mother Eleanor watched our house and brought in the mail. This is the kind of reciprocal relationship that Moll suggests needs to occur between children's home and school families.

Visit Students' Homes

Moll feels that teachers must visit students' homes. We need to get out of the power relationship that the school represents. By visiting children's homes, we increase our chances of becoming real friends. We're more likely to be able to engage parents in participating in long-term curricular studies as partners and mentors to our students.

Working–class families and children from historically oppressed groups deserve the best that education has to offer. Moll observes that often these are the children who are given the most reductionist, skill-and-drill curriculum. Instead of having a literacy-rich environment with many opportunities for talk, reading, and writing, these children are often given endless workbook pages to fill out.

This is especially unfortunate for these children. Talking about the people and ideas they learn about in books is an important way, Moll believes, for students to mediate between their own knowledge and the wider world. He is frustrated that the best literacy instruction seems to be withheld from these children with the implication that they are not as "bright" as other kids, particularly white Americans of European origin.

> The transformative potential of funds of knowledge is debunking ideas of working-class, language-minority households as lacking worthwhile knowledge and experiences. These households, and by implication, these communities, are often viewed solely as places from which children must be saved and rescued, rather than places that, along with problems (as in all communities), contain valuable knowledge and experiences that can foster the children's development. (Moll 1994, p. 444)

Although Moll is eloquent on this subject, his frustration comes through clearly when he ponders the educational fate of these children.

> To be frank, we also lament that we have to spend so much of our careers documenting competence, when it should simply be assumed, suggesting that "language minority" students have the intellectual capabilities of any other children, when it should simply be acknowledged, and proposing instructional arrangements that capitalize fully on the many strengths they bring into classrooms, when it should simply be their right. (Moll, 1994, p. 454)

Julie Maciejewski and Marge O'Martin teach at Wilson School in Cicero, Illinois. They try to make their classrooms warm and inviting places where children feel safe enough to take risks in their learning. Both rooms are filled with children's literature. A variety of the children's artwork hangs from the ceiling of Marge's room. The children in both rooms write and publish many books each month. The teachers try to get to know the students and make personal connections.

One day Julie heard the boys in her classroom talking about Jason's upcoming sleep-over birthday party. "Am I invited?" she asked.

"You never come to our houses," the boys said.

"You'll never come," said Jason.

"You better watch out," she teased.

At first it was just talk, but then Julie began to think about it. She saw this as a way to visit his home and get to know her students in another way. So she called Jason's mother and together they developed their plan.

The birthday party started at eight o'clock that night. The boys arrived and started watching videos and playing games. At nine o'clock, Julie arrived carrying her sleeping bag in her hand. Jason's mother let her in, and Julie walked into the room filled with her students. Jason looked at her in disbelief. The boys gathered around her in shock. After a few minutes they invited her to join in their games.

When Jason's mom announced that it was time for bed, Julie put on her Dr. Denton's pajamas and got into her sleeping bag. "I think they were terrified that I was going to stay the whole night. A little while later though, she went home. "I got to know my students in a different way that night." They trusted her in a new way. Julie felt it was one of the most beneficial things she could have done. Not every teacher has to go to students' birthday parties, but we do need to make connections to the children's culture. Sometimes students face situations that teachers and administrators have little experience with.

Dealing with Gangs

This is my fourth year working in the Cicero district. I've visited this school several times before. Each time there have been many events coinciding with my visits. Sometimes there are police interviewing the kids, sometimes distressed parents. Even with the many interpreters and Spanish speakers in the school, it is not always possible to communicate with the parents. I was not always aware of the problems.

When I first started consulting in Cicero, some of my friends and colleagues asked if I wasn't scared to drive into that area. No, I wasn't scared. As a professor and an educational consultant, I drive all over the city. I've lived here all my life. I know the area. But as I'm becoming part of the community, I'm in tune with more of the kind of talk that teaches me to look carefully at my surroundings. Three of the schools have recently had drive-by shootings either right in front of the school or in the parking lot. These shootings took place during the day, right after dismissal. Fortunately, no one was hurt during those three encounters. This contributes to the dangerous perception, but it is still relatively safe during the day.

The principal explains some cartoon drawings to me. They have been done by some of the boys. "These are gang symbols. The symbols change so quickly, you couldn't possibly keep up with all of them. But over the years, I've learned a lot about gangs," she tells me. "For instance, look at these two pictures of the rabbits. They look similar, but they are two different gangs. Sometimes it's as subtle as the direction of the rabbit, or if an ear is up or down, or the number of dots connected to it."

As we are talking, a fifth-grade boy enters her office. He's suspected of being a gang member. "He looks so young," I murmur.

Gang symbols jotted in notebook.

"Recruiting for the gangs starts early," Debi replies. They recruit kids as young as third grade. By fifth grade many of them are gang members."

"What do they have to do to become gang members?" I ask.

"The boys are beat up."

"What about the girls?" I ask.

"The girls are usually gang-banged by the boys."

We sit in silence for a while. "I know, it's awful," she says. "A lot of these kids are from Roman Catholic families. It's a conflict. These girls want to be good and do what their families expect of them, but some of them feel they have to join the gangs to be protected. The reality of the streets is that you have to walk in groups on your way home. You don't ever want to find yourself alone on the streets."

"How do the gangs get kids to join?" I ask.

Debi looks at me a minute before answering my question. "If a gang targets someone, let's say in this case they want Carlo to join, they have various strategies they can use. They can accidentally bump into him for no reason, push him, shove him, and it's unprovoked. Carlo might walk down the hall and a group of boys are just staring at him, or making snide remarks. They might approach Carlo and say that Antonio is saying bad things about him, and isn't he going to do anything about it? The gang might be trying to get Antonio in the gang, too, and are saying the same things to Antonio. Pretty soon Carlo passes Antonio in the hall and they glare at each other. This is how it begins."

"How many kids in this school join gangs?" I ask. "Does everyone join?"

Debi shakes her head. "The vast majority of the kids are not in gangs in this school. Many kids are able to resist them. Others aren't interested. The gangs aren't interested in those they think are nerds or losers. We try everything we can think of to make this school a safe place for all children. You're not in a gang when you come to school. This year we instituted uniforms as a way to combat the gang colors. Things have calmed down quite a bit. We can help kids fight the gangs and still protect them."

It's a two-way street. The more we learn about our students' cultures, the better we can help them make connections to the culture of the school. Some ways that teachers and schools can get involved with the community are shared in following chapters. Hearing the stories of our colleagues can also be powerful for both our students and ourselves. Ultimately, we want our students to be able to celebrate both their culture and their lives.

How Gangs Have Affected
My Life.

In my past I have lived
around gangs and every night I
would always hear shooting and
how they would do their drive
by shooting. I was very scaried.
They would go shooting who ever
was in the wrong place. I would
never go outside when the gangs
were out because they would
always start shooting or beat
someone up.

Then they would also
shoot for someone's different Identification
Certain gangs have different Identification
They would have their colors a different
way, they have a certain kind of earing
to wear, or clothing, hats, people who their
dot on the opposite side would get
shoot, chased, or beat up. Whoever wears
different identification than their gang
accepts, that person would get beat up or
killed.

Also gangs hang around a
certain place or corner. On those

corner they would represent their gang. Sometimes they would sale drugs on the corner that they are standing at. If they ere not saling the drugs their smoking it. They try to sale it to little kids. Some gangs who really do care about how little kid is they would say no. Also they wouldn't shoot, or represent they probably take you home and then go drive by shooting, represent, or stand on their corner.

Gangs are people who really don't care what happens to other people as long as it's not them or their family. If your in their way you will go down too along with the person their after.

Writing about our lives.

That's what Elizabeth Palacios does. A sixth-grade teacher in Debi's school, she creates a classroom that celebrates Hispanic culture. Her classroom is bright and beautiful, with artwork by major Hispanic artists as well as her students. Her students have been discussing *Friends from the Other Side*, by Gloria Anzalduc. It's a story about illegal immigrants and it's generated a heated discussion in her bilingual class. "Why can't anyone come to

Dear Second Graders,

I heard about what happened to your friend and I feel very sorry and angry that someone could be hurt or killed leaving their house or buying ice cream. Nothings safe now.

I hope that the people who did this get caught and get a good punishment. Also, I hope that what happened to Marisa doesn't happen to you or anyone else you know.

Very Sorry,

Elizabeth

Consoling younger students after the death of their classmate.

the United States?" "Why is the family in hiding?" Their questions are leading them to further inquiry. "Let's add the author to our list," suggests Maria. Prominently on the chalkboard is the list they've been compiling throughout the year. It lists all their favorite Hispanic authors. Many of them are adult authors like Sandra Cisneros. "Have you read *The House on Mango Street?*" one of the students asks me. When I tell him that I have, he beams with pride. "Did you know we had so many wonderful writers?" he asks. "I want to read them all."

Hose Torres also teaches in Cicero. After he moved his family from Mexico to the Chicago area, he went to work in a factory. He dreamed of getting an education, and went to school at night until he received his college diploma. Teaching is a dream he always wanted, but never believed was a possibility. Hose tells his story to his students. He wants them to know his story, and that their dreams can come true, too. It's through talk, reflection, and inquiry that we can begin to teach for multicultural understanding.

"That's the thing," Margo Cairney tells me. "I feel like our kids start with so many strikes against them. We have wonderful, bright, talented stu-

Dear President Maltese,

What Bugs Me about Cicero

I am going to tell you what bugs me about Cicero. I live in an apartment and there is a little place where there is a few trees. Anyway, they just throw their garbage in front of the apartment, right by the trees. Maybe we could get a garbage can on 26th St What do you think?

Crystal Vela
Burnham school
Rm 212

Cleaning up the environment.

dents who would flourish if they lived in a wealthy suburb with strong technology support and families who visit museums and have the money to provide the extras. I feel like our kids have so many strikes against them. They have limited funding in their schools. They don't have the privilege of safe neighborhoods. Their parents aren't able to take them to the museums. Many have limited ability to speak English. They come to school so much

SERVICE HOURS

By Courtney Valent

Cicero has alot of people that need help and alot of garbage that needs to be picked up. The older people who live around Cicero are not going to pick it up every day. So why don't us children form a team and go out every day or one time a week and pick up all that trash. This is a question for my class room 212 for a very long time, until now when we have made those teams. There is one team that goes to the Nursing home and one that goes and cleans the parks and one that visits Homeless Shelters. My class room 212 has worked very hard to make this happen and we hope that if people see us doing these service projects and see how it helps people and the environment maybe they will help too.

Reflecting on the service project.

less prepared than their counterparts in the wealthier schools. And yet, the students want to learn. They engage in literacy learning eagerly. They love the books and write incredible stories and make great progress. And then they take the standardized tests and do abysmally. The children feel defeated and we defeated."

Margo relates this to an incident that Annie Dillard so poignantly writes about in her book, *An American Childhood*. Annie's teacher had brought in a cocoon with a moth inside in a small jar. The jar was too small for the moth. After moths hatch, they need enough room to fully spread their wings so that the blood reaches their veins and enables them to fly. If this doesn't happen during the critical period, the moth can't fly and eventually dies. Annie Dillard remembers watching with her class as the moth emerged, but couldn't spread it's wings. They watched it hop along the driveway.

"That's how I feel my students are," said Margo. "Incredible kids with clipped wings." Their wings have been stunted by society, by injustice, by lack of resources, and in some cases by a lack of caring.

Many of the kids who are outsiders have suffered in some of these ways. These children have suffered from the five factors of oppression (Young 1990): exploitation, marginalization, powerlessness, cultural imperialism, and violence. It is our responsibility to help them reach their full potential.

Recently researchers found that children who grew up witnessing violence were *two to nine* times more likely to be violent themselves. We need to provide an antidote to violence and inequity. We may not be able to change the world, but we can affect our classrooms. We have to teach not only the facts, but what they mean. Literacy provides a map, a way for us to make sense of the world. The world may be unpredictable and violent, but it is also hopeful and inspiring. When we really see and acknowledge our students' realities, we provide a vehicle for expression. When students live in classrooms that nurture them and promote opportunities for all students, multiple possibilities open up for them. We can make a difference, and our students learn that they can make a difference, too.

7

Talk, Reflection, and Inquiry: Three Key Components of the Literacy Process

Talk

Talk, reflection, and inquiry are three key components of the literacy process. As classroom teachers, we rely on talk to get the work of the curriculum done. In recent years, our understanding of talk has deepened and we've worked consciously to provide children opportunities to "talk through" their understandings in many cooperative group situations. Douglas Barnes (1976) showed us the importance of students having time to think through their understandings, and called the process "exploratory talk." This is an important concept. Students need to take risks in their thinking to make conceptual leaps. If we rush them, or demand a certain answer, we're more likely to get what Barnes calls "final-draft talk." This is the polished, correct-answer talk that we so often expect. But for students to make those deep connections, they need time to rehearse, to sound awkward, to try on new ideas and make their own conclusions.

Time to Think

Time is an essential ingredient. So often the pace in our classrooms goes so fast that students can barely raise their hands before questions are answered and new questions tossed out. We have to change qualitatively our class-room atmosphere so that thinking is honored. We're not looking for the fastest answer but for understanding. Time also gives us the opportunity to support students' growth in their Zone of Proximal Development through Scaffolding. This is an important concept and the essence of education.

Scaffolding and The Zone of Proximal Development

Through talk, we're able to assess and teach. Scaffolding and the Zone of Proximal Development are two key concepts that are involved in this process. The Zone of Proximal Development is a concept developed by the Russian psychologist Vygotsky in the early part of this century. The Zone of Proximal Development (or ZPD) is the next level of cognitive development a child might reach with the support of adults or more accomplished peers. Bruner's idea of Scaffolding explains how we as caregivers help children move into their individual zones.

Observations

Scaffolding begins with the careful observation of children. We watch them and offer only the amount of support they need, and no more. Scaffolds are temporary structures providing support when needed and withdrawn as soon as children reach the next level. Three conditions are present during this process. First, children take the initiative and take control of their learning. Second, we provide just the information that is needed at the moment, and third, once the new level has been achieved, the child demonstrates this and does not return to the previous level. Instead, we "up the ante," or raise the scaffold to a higher conceptual level.

A good way to picture this is to imagine one of the many routines that are present during children's early years. For instance, there is the eating routine, the bath routine, and in many homes the book-reading routine. Often, before children go to bed, we read them a story. Even the youngest child has some control over this situation. Have you ever noticed how children choose the same book over and over again? This actually allows them to process the beautiful language in the book, over and over again, analyzing and making sense of it. Even a baby can exercise control over the book reading event by chewing on the book or shutting it, effectively ending the book-reading session.

Providing information.

The second condition of scaffolding involves our ability to provide just the information the child needs. So if we're reading *Brown Bear, Brown Bear,* for example, the nine-month–old baby may point to the bear and say "bah." This encourages us, and often we praise the child. When the child is older and says, "bear," we are again excited and say something like, "Yes, it says 'Brown Bear.' " At this point we're nudging the child to continue moving forward intellectually. Our previous interactions would be inappropriate. As adults, we automatically know how to scaffold children's learning. It is something that is built into our species. That's the good news about Scaffolding. We already know how to do it. We need to take this unconscious knowledge and raise it to the conscious level when we're working with students in classrooms.

Scaffolding in classrooms is complicated. Meeting the needs of a group of students is particularly challenging. How can teachers possibly find the time to observe students and scaffold their learning when there are so many children who are at so many different levels. Some teachers give up in frustration, never having tried. Others reinvent Scaffolding to suit their purposes. Scaffolding can't be done by providing one lesson to the whole class and deciding what you're going to scaffold ahead of time. Instead it is a minute–by–minute operation, based on students' needs, not teacher's plans.

Scaffolding in the Zone of Proximal Development is the essence of learning, and the core of literacy learning. This is how children learn and how we best teach. So much of this work is accomplished through talk. This is why it is so important for students to talk in our classrooms. Exploratory talk is crucial for children's cognitive growth, as is wait time.

Reflection

Wait Time

Many teachers have heard about wait–time research. A large body of research supports the idea that if teachers wait three to five seconds after asking a question or before calling on a student, higher-level learning will occur. Even more importantly, if teachers can wait three to five seconds when students have stopped talking, more complex ideas will develop. Wait time sounds easy to accomplish, but in reality it's quite difficult. During wait time, the teacher must be completely quiet. This means saying nothing, not even offering encouragement or praise. The minute we start talking, students' thinking is interrupted and thoughts are lost. The rewards of using wait time in classrooms are great.

Don Graves (1994) talks about the pace and atmosphere during the writing workshop as being qualitatively different than often occurs. It should be slower to encourage reflection. A classroom where wait time occurs is what we should strive for most of the time. The only time wait time is inappropriate is when children are memorizing items or doing things by rote.

A problem with using wait time is that teachers have such a difficult time applying it. Even though three to five seconds sounds like such a short amount of time, it still is too long for most teachers to use in school. Teachers may start out with the best of intentions, but then abandon wait time when they feel pressured. I watch myself during the many times that I offer demonstrations in classroom. For example, in one second–grade classroom, Matthew read his ghost story aloud. One child asked, "Why did the ghost have red eyes?" Matthew sat quietly saying nothing. I noticed my heart pounding and the students and all the other teachers watching him and watching me. Should I step in? Should I say something? Is this taking too much time? What if he has nothing to say? What if he didn't even hear the answer?

It's all I can do to restrain myself and not talk, yet each time, I'm rewarded. Matthew speaks. "The reason the ghost had red eyes is because he is mean and his eyes glowed with anger." I'm so pleased that I restrained myself, but I go through this every time.

Wondering how much wait time we use socially, I tried an experiment. One of my friends had won a trip to the racetrack, which was a great place for the investigation. Holding my stopwatch under the table and out of sight, my plan was to note the time between each interaction. Before I could even push the button on my stopwatch, someone else began to speak. This went on the whole afternoon. Wait time was measured only twice during the entire afternoon.

This really shouldn't be too surprising because it was a social situation, not an academic one. But it does point out the fast pace at which our society moves. We don't provide much reflection time during our days. Therefore, it's especially important that we offer it in academic situations. However, it does partially explain why it is difficult to institute it in our classrooms. If we rarely use wait time and/or are uncomfortable with it, it's going to be harder to initiate in our classrooms. Our students may also be unfamiliar and uncomfortable with it. They've been taught to talk fast and raise their hands quickly. So a classroom that honors wait time and reflection could be a radical departure for most students.

Over the past thirty years, Mary Budd Rowe (1987), Nathan Swift (1988), and many others have shown the effectiveness of wait time across many curriculums, ages and situations. Both Dr. Rowe and Dr. Swift spent time showing teachers how to monitor and improve their wait time usage. Dr. Rowe was able to show teachers how to monitor their wait time performance (through complicated means), but teachers' use of it dropped after the training. Dr. Swift invented a machine that would flash when the wait time period was over, but again it worked best when the teachers had use of the machine. Without the machine, teachers had difficulty continuing to use wait time.

Both researchers focused on teaching only the teachers, and not the students. Dr. Swift postulated that if the students were also taught how to use wait time, it would be easier to institute wait time in the classroom. I agree, and think that you can take it even one step further. Children can benefit from using wait time with each other, especially in reflective times like conferences during writing workshop.

When I teach students to use wait time, I do it in conjunction with teaching them to conference. I tell the students that during conferences we want their most reflective answers, not the first thing that comes to their minds. For this to happen, they need to take the time to think of a reflective answer or a reflective question. I don't call this wait time, but thinking time. I point out that at any moment during a productive conference you might see both people thinking and no one talking. Especially during the beginning of the year, I highlight examples of thinking time during conferences and whenever they occur. So through demonstrations and reflections, thinking time becomes a natural part of the school day.

Kidwatching and Reflection

Thinking and reflection are important for students, but they are also important for teachers. What are we doing when we work with kids? We can use this thinking time to hone our observational skills so we can specifically help and scaffold children's learning. Informal records are important in classrooms. As teachers, we are constantly thinking, observing, and nudging our students forward. We need our informal records to help us continue the scaffolding cycle. We can't always remember what we did two weeks ago, and though we know Teresa made progress, we're less able to remember the specifics as time goes by. By keeping records throughout the day, we're able to document both our students' progress and our own journey as we help them.

Often, teachers call a small group of children to work with them in reading. The kids have their books and the teacher watches them. What happens next? Every time children read aloud, teachers should be watching. How are they reading? Haltingly or without problems? Are they laughing if the text is humorous? Do they lack interest? What happens if children don't know words? Does the teacher simply say the correct word, or does she watch to see what strategies the child will use?

There are many problems with telling students the correct words. Perhaps the greatest problem is that it prevents us from Kidwatching and takes away our opportunities for Scaffolding. How can we scaffold if we don't know what the children are doing? Every time kids read, we need to watch them. Even if we only have a minute. What's happening when they read? Do they ever go back and try to make sense of the text? Are their substitutions appropriate? Are children able to make sense of the text anyway? Can they retell their selections showing comprehension of the text? By keeping an informal miscue analysis, teachers have valuable information that can help them to support student learning.

Kidwatching (Goodman 1996) leads to reflection for both the teachers and the students. When we invite students to reflect on their work, they add additional insights. For example, if we share with students some of the things we've observed during miscue analysis, we get their interpretations of what they did. This is part of retrospective miscue analysis (Goodman and Marek 1996). Encouraging students to reflect on their literacy processes is important and has often been neglected in the past. The use of portfolios is one of the ways that teachers have tried to incorporate student insights.

The Pillars of Literacy
Reflection is inherent to all the Pillars of Literacy (Crafton 1991).

The Pillars of Literacy
1. Whole to Part Learning
2. The Social Construction of Meaning
3. Authentic Reading and Writing Experiences
4. Risk-Taking and Approximation
5. Student Responsibility for Learning

Literacy begins with the experience of reading or writing. We read a book or write a poem. This doesn't mean that we don't teach the skills and strategies that are needed to help us read or write. Actually, it means that we teach these skills and strategies better than we have in the past. For instance, phonics and spelling instruction make sense in the context of assisting children to write. Helping children make the connection between sounds and symbols is much better phonics teaching than asking them to fill out worksheets with pictures so obscure that even the teacher has to look up the answer to name the object in the picture.

One of the most important things we've learned from literacy instruction is the importance of the learners in constructing meaning. I may have one interpretation and you may have another. The power of our working together is that by sharing our views of the world, we both enrich and expand all of our understandings of the world. This is extremely important in teaching for social justice. For students who come from similar backgrounds, it may be through their interaction with multicultural literature that they confront stereotypes and learn tolerance. Sometimes we have to get beyond our own world view to do this.

Authentic reading and writing experiences are meaningful and purposeful. We need to read and write about issues that are important in the world. The classroom structures that support this kind of work include student choice of the books they read, literature discussions, and writing workshops. Many fine books have been written about these processes. The first step in using literacy to teach for equity and social justice is to have these vehicles in place in your classroom.

Students need to feel safe enough to take risks when they talk, read, write, and learn. This is a simple statement, but very powerful. If risk is encouraged, it's okay to sound confused and make mistakes. It can be very scary when learning something new. We have to feel safe enough to feel confused. Experiencing cognitive dissonance can be terrifying. We have to know it's okay not to know all the answers.

Student responsibility for learning means more than requiring students to do their work. Literacy should be so compelling that students take charge of their work. They choose their direction and their books. Students determine their questions and their assignments. They choose their writing topics and control their writing process. When children conference with others, they choose the direction their written manuscripts will take. These are the Pillars of Literacy that are necessary, and the foundation of teaching equity and social justice.

Inquiry

The Authoring Circles and Inquiry

If the Pillars of Literacy are the foundation, then the Authoring Cycle and inquiry-based instruction provide the necessary structure in which literacy can flourish. Carolyn Burke, Jerome Harste, and Kathy Short (1996) have written about both and provided us with both the practical and theoretical frameworks. The Authoring Cycle represents the cycle in which both reading and writing projects are lived, from the beginning

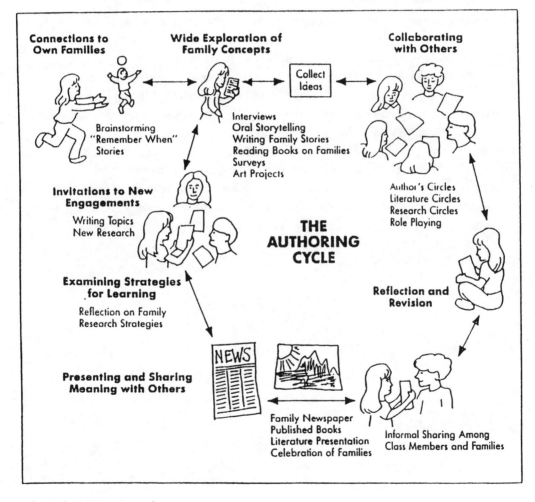

The Authoring/Inquiry cycle.

(Burke, C., Harste, J., and K. Short, 1991)

invitations that are offered in our classrooms through the journey of coming to know.

In this representation of the Authoring Cycle, students are making connections and exploring families. Notice how the arrows point in both directions, emphasizing the recursive nature of this process. Reflection and revision, although listed in just one area, take place at every juncture. This cycle works for reading, writing, and inquiry. Our questions arise from our experiences, our invitations offered to us, and by our previous work. As we begin our reading, our questions arise. As we write, we share our manuscripts in process. Kathy Short and Jerry Harste are calling the reflection section "attending to difference." This gets at the notion that real learning occurs from differences, not similarities. So even though diversity may be hard for us to live by, it's necessary for us to flourish. Reflection helps us make sense of the differences and to consolidate knowledge.

Presenting and sharing meaning with others offers us opportunities to articulate in some way part of what we've learned. This isn't meant to be a formal presentation as much as an opportunity to share some of our learning with the class. As we reflect on our learning, we have new questions that lead to new investigations. So the Authoring Cycle becomes the Inquiry Cycle. Questions from our previous engagements lead to new questions that begin the cycle all over again. It is through this cycle that both learning and literacy flourishes. And it is within this literacy environment that students can begin to examine issues of equity, multicultural diversity, and social justice. In the next chapter, we'll look more closely at the reflection part of the cycle.

8 | Learning to Hear Each Other

Sarah says:

> This has been the best year of my life because I've had the best teachers.
> This year we learned in a different way than all the other years. We do a
> lot more group things. Like last year, we sat in a group, and once in a while
> we might compare answers on a math page or something. This year we *re-
> ally* work in groups, instead of just sitting in a group. Our teachers work to-
> gether and they show us how to do that. They're members of the group
> and to each other.

Sarah is talking about her sixth-grade teachers, Arlene Langley and
Lisa Forsythe. Arlene and Lisa have worked together in Downers Grove, a
suburb west of Chicago, for the last four years. They have removed the wall
between their adjacent classrooms so that they can teach the fifty students
cooperatively as one unit.

Arlene and Lisa share a common belief system. They agree that school
should be meaningful and purposeful, and that students should have choices
in their learning. They believe in collaboration both for their students and

themselves. The students in their classroom work together throughout the day. The teachers' collaboration is central to their teaching.

The students' relationships with their teachers developed and deepened over time as they came to understand their teachers' belief systems. Jenny, a student who had recently moved to the area, had previously experienced difficulty in school. She shared her feelings about both teachers.

JENNY: Mrs. Langley's really great. I think it's because she has eight kids. She helped me a lot. In the beginning I had a little hard time trying to respect Mrs. Forsythe, cause I have brothers older than she is and I don't have to respect them. So I had just a little hard time respecting her, but I learned to.

RH: Why are they good teachers?

JENNY: Because they care. Most people wouldn't care. Like if I'm upset, they know how to calm me down. And they know how to talk to me. They just are there. They are better teachers than the ones who get their paycheck and they don't take any problems home.

RH: So this year was better than you expected it to be partly because of the teachers really caring about you. What have you learned this year about yourself as a learner?

JENNY: That I can change. I didn't think I could, but I did.

Jenny doubted her ability to adjust to her new school and classmates, and credits her teachers for helping her make this transition. Arlene and Lisa are sensitive to the students and get involved in their lives. Relationships are important, and both teachers take the time to understand students and work with them individually.

All fifty students are taught by both Arlene and Lisa. Both teachers are involved in every project that occurs throughout the school day. One teacher begins a sentence, and the other ends it. One teacher may start a mini-lesson, and then stop and help an individual. The other teacher then continues the mini-lesson. Arlene and Lisa negotiate this change in front of their students. Their students learn to collaborate by participating in classroom life.

It's often hard to locate Arlene or Lisa in the classroom. They blend in because of the learner role they assume. They may join literature circles as participants, or help individual students through writing conferences. They work with students continuously throughout the school day, sharing their questions with their students and serving as co-learners in the classroom. Math, science, and social studies are often integrated through inquiry projects and focused study groups. Students can be observed working on computers and conferring with their teachers before school, at lunch and recess, and after school.

I had worked with both teachers before this six-week study began, and was working with them again as a participant–observer who hoped to study students' evaluation of their learning. I was interested in the range of learning that took place throughout the day. I observed and interviewed students during their writing workshops and a variety of inquiry projects. I participated in literature discussions and focused study groups. I also talked with children during math and art and science. Although self-evaluation was present in the classroom, we became increasingly aware of just how often, and how much earlier in the process, it really occurs. We also came to understand its power to complete the learning cycle.

Forming a Thought Collective

Thought collectives are like think tanks. It is the kind of generative and deep thinking that students can do in groups. Rather than group work that focuses on surface questions, thought collectives require students to be analytical and reflective. Forming thought collectives is a shared goal in this classroom. Students work across the curriculum on many projects in groups, but cooperation is only the first step. Collaboration is necessary for thought collectives to develop. Students learn to collaborate by sharing a commitment to their joint goals, by valuing diversity, and by supporting risk-taking (Short and Burke 1991). In thought collectives, perspectives are established in relationship to others. Students move beyond individual reflections to joint insights and understandings. In order for thought collectives to grow, the group needs to establish a focused intent. Members share perspectives, which are listened to and incorporated into the group's joint understanding. Reflecting and revaluing are necessary for new values to be implemented.

Sarah, for example, was an enthusiastic student, eager to share her insights with me. In Sarah's life as a student, she demonstrated the kind of reflective learning that Crafton (1991) describes, in that she:

1. Self-initiates
2. Problem-solves
3. Reflectively evaluates her learning
4. Collaborates and shows concern for others
5. Engages in complex thinking strategies

It's significant that when Sarah assessed her learning, she discussed collaboration. I asked her, "What have you learned this year about yourself as a learner?"

> Well, I can work individually or in a group. It depends on what I'm doing. Like in math. I prefer to work individually because I'm quick in math. I can do the things quickly. But then in something like social studies it's fun to get different opinions, like kind of a debate to decide, not really who's right, but just to compare thinking. So it's fun to do that.

Becoming Self-Evaluators

Evaluation is integral to learning. We need to reflect and revise our thinking while we are in the process of learning. Burke (Burke and Short 1991) points out that until recently, evaluation has been focused in one area only. Standardized tests have often been the only means used to measure learning. Burke (p. 67) defines tests as artifacts that are found at the society level of evaluation. These tests are the remnants of a culture that sees evaluation as a measure outside the learning process. A child's knowledge is tested by an examination someone else constructs for the purpose of determining what the student has learned. This notion, that evaluation consists of externally imposed tests that measure students learning, is predominant in the United States.

Rather than tests, authentic evaluation measures the actual process of reading and writing. The movement toward authentic forms of evaluation reflects dissatisfaction with learning that is assessed outside of the learning context, and with little consideration for the individual. Tests represent only one aspect of evaluation. And, as Burke's model indicates, the possibilities are so much richer.

Carolyn Burke integrates evaluation throughout the curricular process. Until recently, the importance of students' self-evaluation, while included in the learning process, has been overlooked, thus missing important opportunities for growth and learning.

Conflict, Reflection, and Inquiry

During my participation in this classroom, I was especially interested in the evaluation that occurred earlier in the students' inquiry projects. Sarah, Areila, and Sue were participating in a focused study group. They had formed this group based on their shared interest in a topic. They had decided to study the role of religion in the Middle Ages. Sarah was a confi-

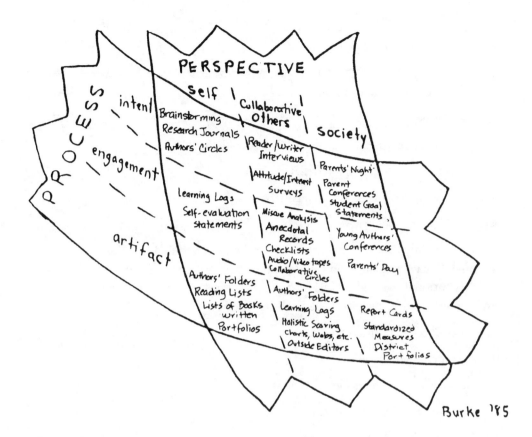

Burke's model of curriculum evaluation.

dent learner, as her previous reflections reveal. Areila often agreed with Sarah and followed her lead. Sarah and Areila sat near each other. Sue sat farther away, alone and somber. The girls were deciding how to present their project to the class. When I joined the triangle, they were in the middle of an argument:

SARAH:: We took a majority vote and, Sue, you lost.

SUE: Well obviously you guys don't want to do it. So it's the easiest way to get out of it.

AREILA: Well we're not obligated to tell everything about that. All we need to do is. . . .

SARAH: I think we need to, that's not the most important thing, we have to talk about the most important thing.

SUE: Well, I'm talking about how they would steal and everything like that. You would think, 'Oh well the church people wouldn't steal or do bad things like that.'

SARAH: Well, I think we would tell how the church was so important to them and they did have the Ten Commandments to not steal.

SUE: But they did!

SARAH: Excuse me, excuse me, excuse me. That would, should show . . .

AREILA: I don't care what the church says.

SARAH: But really the church was so important in their lives.

SUE: The church was doing it.

At this point, I didn't understand the problem of the group. Sue was emotional, her voice rising and falling. The other two girls were calm and seemingly rational. I wondered what Sue's problem was. There was a long silence and then all three girls began talking at once.

SUE: You guys aren't understanding.

SARAH: Churches don't steal.

SUE: On the way there, they stole food and stuff!

AREILA: On the way there they stole food?

SUE: (Emphatically) People of the church!

I began to understand the issue they were discussing. Sue's research had led her to the discovery that the Crusaders raided and stole in the name of religion. Sarah and Areila's research had focused on the ethical underpinnings of the Crusaders' religion. People should not steal. Yet Sue was saying they did. Could Sue make her point, and would Sarah and Areila be able to hear it?

SUE: You don't have to go making jokes about it. Every idea that I have, you guys won't do it.

SARAH: That's not true. We have used some of your ideas.

SUE: Which ideas?

SARAH: The one about speaking.

SUE: This is not about . . .

AREILA: How can we put that in and make it fun?

Areila seemed especially concerned that the presentation of the project be something fun. This was a cause for concern because the topic under discussion was anything but fun. It was serious and difficult to grasp. Sue, feeling frustrated, continued to raise her voice, accentuate her words, and accuse the others of not listening to her.

SUE: You're just talking everything down.

SARAH: We need help. We're a group, but we have to work as a group.

SUE: Every time I say something, you guys don't listen!

At this point the group looked at me with frustration. I suggested that we step back and reflect on the process and the progress of the group. I asked them to describe the conflict.

SARAH: I think Sue is asking us to put in how they got to Jerusalem, how they stole, and we don't want to put that in, because we interpreted it differently than Sue did, and we decided they stole once they were there, rather than on the way there.

AREILA: We're trying to get the main idea here, and Sue is putting in the minor details, which aren't too important.

SUE: This is what I would do. On the way there they, the people would steal or anything that they did, the church people, the popes, everyone, they stole on the way there.

I wasn't sure how to help them. Before I could ask them to evaluate their group process, I wanted to make sure that we were in agreement about the area of conflict. So I acted as an observer, trying to summarize and restate the issue:

RH: So we have a real ethical problem here. Sue thinks it's very important to tell the truth about the whole thing, and she thinks that if you tell about the stealing when they are in Jerusalem, you're leaving out a major part of the story. What I'm hearing is that you don't want to put in the stealing part. You're just going to talk about it when they get there. So you're going to talk about the stealing, but you're not going to tell the whole story about how they stole and took all those things on the way.

The girls nodded their heads in agreement. I felt that we could begin the process of reflection.

RH: I want to stop us now and take time to reflect on this. There's a real conflict that's unsolved. The first thing I want to ask is how you think this work is going.

SARAH: I think it's not going too well.

RH: Why is it not going too well?

Areila: We have different ideas about this and we're having a relative hard time agreeing with each other. We have different opinions and we're not trying to understand each other that well.

RH: Sue, what do you think? How do you think this group is going?

SUE: It was going pretty good, up until today.

RH: How was it going good, up until today?

SUE: We were all working together.

RH: What's the problem with today?

SUE: Well, probably my ideas. It's not what they want to do. They're not listening to what I had in my notes, and then throwing it out.

Areila's conciliatory statement seemed to affect the mood of the group. Sue was willing to concede that the group had worked well together, and was less emotional when explaining her position. I wanted the girls to realize the importance of evaluating their progress, or lack of it, while they were still working together and could have the opportunity and the time to change. Here was an opportunity to move them beyond simple remembering. I asked them, "How can thinking about how the group is going make it better?"

SARAH: Right now, it's not going too good, and we can, like, listen to each other more carefully, which is, I think, what our problem is, kinda. Also, we can be more flexible.

Sarah and Areila were so uncomfortable with Sue's information that they chose to reject it, believing that she was wrong. I wanted to nudge them toward a recognition of their discomfort (inconsistencies) with the conflicting information and toward revaluing this data. I wanted to show them that inclusion of alternate perspectives was key to collaborative group work. I observed, "So you think that by listening to each other more carefully, and by being more flexible (considering other perspectives), you can resolve this and eliminate further conflicts."

AREILA: I know that you think the part about stealing on the way is important, and we can include it, we just didn't understand how important it was.

SARAH: Maybe what we could do to put it in, we could say. It took over a hundred years for the Crusaders to reach Jerusalem. As they went there, they demolished cities and towns, and . . . I don't know what else.

SUE: That was what I was trying to say before. That was my idea before, but you weren't listening to it carefully.

Now that Sarah and Areila had conceded, they expected Sue to understand their viewpoint.

SARAH: Don't take this as an insult. Wait. When you talk, I think maybe, to help us understand you better, you should state your ideas more clearly, because . . .

SUE: Well you didn't . . .

SARAH: And another thing we can do is to stop interrupting each other, cause that's a big thing, we keep interrupting each other and getting in fights and stuff.

The girls had returned to their verbal sparring. However, they realized it quickly, and continued to reflect on their interactions. Areila noticed that they interrupted each other, pointed it out, and suggested that they stop it. I wanted them to deepen their evaluation. I asked, "What made you decide to include the raiding along the way?"

SARAH: Because we were being more flexible.

RH: Do you think if I wasn't here you would have decided this?

SARAH: Probably not.

RH: So how did my role change what happened here?

SARAH: You asked us to reflect on what we were saying.

RH: Why is it important to evaluate what you're doing while you're doing it?

SUE: Maybe sometimes you just have to compare before people can see, so when you reflect, then you can kind of compare it.

SARAH: I think it's important to reflect, because in this situation, Areila and I didn't realize what we were doing. We didn't realize what Sue was saying. So since we thought about it more, we didn't end up saying 'No, we don't like that.' And we decided that it was a good idea, and we did need to say it.

AREILA: I think I agree with Sarah. At first we didn't know how important it was. We realized that we were wrong and we gave it some thought.

RH: What have you learned from this—that because of it, you'll do differently next time?

AREILA: I think I will try and put myself in kids' places and think how I would feel if there was something I knew that had to be in there.

SARAH: If we didn't understand what someone is saying, we could stop them and have them repeat the idea. And we could reflect, too.

The discussion ended at this point. I missed an important opportunity to move the girls' thinking beyond their social awareness to inquiry awareness. They were willing to consider alternate points, but they weren't able to deal with the conflicting knowledge. By ignoring the data, the girls didn't have to deal with the inconsistencies caused by alternate perspectives of knowledge.

Underlying Processes in This Classroom

Reflection, collaboration, and inquiry-based evaluation were supported by the underlying process in this classroom. Learning to hear each other was central to the process. This was not an easy task for any of the girls. Next, we needed to move beyond memory to reflection. Third, evaluation was internal to the learning process. Through evaluation, the group moved to a deeper level as a thought collective. Fourth, the individuals were operating within the confines of a thought collective. The shared perspective was formed by the research of each group member.

As I interacted with the sixth-grade students, I realized that there were at least four crucial aspects of evaluation that occurred in this classroom:

1. *Discussion*. The role of discussion was honored and valued. Evaluation wasn't just elicited through writing in learning logs and journals. Much of the evaluation from both the students and the teachers was done orally. To study this, we used tape recorders; transcripts of the discussions provide the central focus of this chapter.
2. *Cooperation*. Collaborative problem-solving was highly valued in this classroom. Therefore, evaluation often highlighted aspects of group work, and how groups might function better. Students were evaluated as a group, not just individually.
3. *Teacher facilitation*. I found my role as another cooperative teacher in the class room quite different and more important than I first imagined. The teacher, as

facilitator, helped the group move ahead when communication broke down. There were times during group work when students were unable to resolve their differences. I acted as a facilitator and helped students to evaluate the process and progress of the group. It was important for some member of the group to assume this function—to move beyond remembering to true reflection.

4. *Continual implementation*. Evaluation is an ongoing process. Not only do we remember and reflect on our learning, we use this information to make change. Therefore, evaluation is important throughout the learning process, *not just at the end*. Reflection leads to action.

Forming Potential Thought Collectives

In Thought Collectives, members progress as thought is made available to the group. The perspective has to be established in *relationship* to others. Pragmatic circumstances, shared life experiences, and significant interests are recognized and matter to the collective. Evaluation helps make change possible and moves thinking forward. Reflection and revaluing are necessary before conflicting data can be examined and new perspectives integrated.

Students need to examine information. There are multiple perspectives on all knowledge. I missed an important opportunity to help the girls move beyond their evaluation of their social awareness to an examination of why it was so difficult for them to accept conflicting research. We might have begun to understand and explore the idea that there are alternate perspectives on all knowledge. This may then have led to new implemented values, and to further study. We also could have shared our inquiry with the classroom, inviting others to reflect with us. I hope that next time I will be able to nudge students further. Thought Collectives offer all of us rich opportunities to grow.

9 | Who Are the Outsiders?

Throughout this book, we've been talking about outsiders. Who are the outsiders? They could be anyone. They could even be you or me. Depending on the situation, any of us may find ourselves on the margin. The difference between students and adults, though, is that children often find themselves in situations over which they have no control, especially in school.

Sharon Murphy and Curt Dudley-Marling warn of the dangers that can befall students in school systems. "The reality is that, for many people, education and hard work are insufficient to surmount the crippling effects of poverty or racial, gender, or religious discrimination" (1997, p.460). Middle– and upper–class children come to school most prepared for success because the school culture most closely matches their home lives. Too often, for children living in poverty, little is done to connect their home experiences with their school lives. "Schools are also implicated in producing and reproducing inequities related to race, class, gender, and language by favoring knowledge and pedagogical practices that privilege the skills and experiences of middle– and upper-middle–class students" (p. 461). Those students who live in poverty are likely to remain outsiders who are overlooked and struggling in our schools.

Murphy and Dudley-Marling note that these children often fail to become literate. "Working to improve the reading of individual students may make a difference in the short term, but long-term change requires the exploration of ways to challenge the racist, classist, sexist, homophobic, and ablest structures of schooling that produced so much failure in the first place, structures that ensure that disproportionate numbers of students from marginalized groups will achieve little economic or social success no matter how literate they become" (p. 467). We need to fight the inequities of society that are already in our classrooms.

Being an outsider isn't necessarily a bad thing. Some children may prefer to spend time by themselves. That's the key, though. Is it the children's wish to be alone, or are they excluded against their will? The children we're focusing on here are those who don't want to be excluded, but are.

"I believe the ultimate outsiders are special education children," says Rose Casement, a teacher in Maine. "They're seen as different and never really become part of the community." These are the children that Rose teaches. "Just because my students have low IQ's doesn't mean they don't have anything to give," she says. Kathy Feldheim, a teacher in Highland Park, Illinois, agrees, adding that the hearing–impaired and physically handicapped children in her school enrich everyone. "I think most people are scared of what they haven't experienced. That's why it's important for kids to be in school with children from lots of different backgrounds. If they grow up with them, they'll understand that there is nothing to be afraid of."

There are many ways that children come to our rooms as outsiders. It might be the group they were born into, especially if it's not the dominant culture of the school. They may be outside the culture because of economic reasons. The racism that some students face may never be acknowledged or understood in the schools. Indeed, poverty and racism are among our greatest social problems. But even when a class is entirely composed of one oppressed race, culture, or economic level, students still can be outsiders to the school culture as, their high delinquent and drop-out rate can attest.

Outsiders come from every racial, cultural, and economic group, or from within the dominant group. Perhaps the outsider in your class is the child who is incredibly shy, or the one who has temper tantrums. Maybe it's the child who has trouble articulating his or her thoughts or can't stop talking. Some children are unpopular because of emotional problems.

Developing Emotional Intelligence

The whole area of emotional intelligence is one that has been generally overlooked by schools. Daniel Goleman (1995) suggests that schools should use situations of conflict as opportunities to learn about controlling emotions. He says that we need to teach children how to develop "character," and emotional literacy should be part of the academic curriculum.

In his book, *The Optimistic Child* (1995), Martin Seligman describes how to do this. He's found that a large number of children are pessimistic, leading to depression at earlier ages than previously assumed. These children often are invisible, or they strike out at others physically. They aren't able to sustain relationships. They might become uncooperative or sullen. Seligman believes that if we teach kids to counter pessimism, many children can avoid depression.

David often gets very frustrated in his fifth–grade classroom. When his teacher, Peggy Nadziejko, sees his frustration mounting, she tries to help him remember to relax, cool down, and figure out the consequences for each alternative behavior he can choose. But this presupposes that David can articulate his anger. Many times he's so angry, he starts screaming and yelling. "He actually lies down and kicks and has a temper tantrum," says Peggy.

"What do you do?" I ask her.

Peggy thinks this over before answering. "I wait until he's all done screaming. Then I tell him to come over and give me a big, tight bear hug. I tell him to squeeze very hard and get the fat off of me."

"Does it work?" I ask her.

"Every time. He calms down and goes back to work."

Linda Bailey, a teacher in the Chicago public schools, believes it's critical that the schools offer a warm, loving atmosphere for children. She believes that hugging is a key component. "At my school, we're allowed to hug the kids everyday. We're even encouraged to. We have one student who was a crack baby and freaks out everyday. The only way he remains sane is through the hugs."

"Perhaps we should have hugging as a goal," reflects teacher Heidi Bleizen. "How about 'pass the hug.' What if we tried to hug every child every day! Imagine the benefits! What would happen if we hugged all the children who ended up in detention each day?"

The students were preparing for a high tea in Peggy Nadziejko's class. This was a special occasion. The students had brewed tea and baked scones from a special recipe. As they were writing their invitations to their mothers and other women who had made a difference in their lives, David had another temper attack. Peggy held him for an especially long time. Finally he was able to verbalize what was wrong. "My mom's not there for me. She doesn't come around. She doesn't care about me. But you are, Mrs. Nadziejko. You care about me, and so does my stepmom." This breakthrough was possible because of all the hard work and hugs that had happened during the year.

Children of Lesbian and Gay Households

There are many kinds of not-so-obvious outsiders in our schools. Children who come from lesbian and gay homes often remain invisible for the whole school experience. They may not appear to suffer socially because no one knows about their home life. Coming out, a major hurdle for most lesbian and gay people, is a problem for children, too.

Amy and Craig are being raised by two mothers. Their mom Luann has been raising the two children with her lifetime partner Lana since Craig was three and Amy was five. While in eighth and sixth grades, they shared some of their experiences with their parents. "It was hard for me," says Craig. I was always worried that if anyone found out, I wouldn't have any friends. So I never talked about Lana. It was like she didn't exist."

Except that she did. Luann worked in the city, so it was Lana who did much of the day–to–day raising of the children. As a teacher, she was home right after school and all summer. She drove the kids to their basketball, baseball, and soccer practices and helped them with their homework.

Both mothers attended the children's conferences. Since Lana was the teacher, she asked a lot of questions. The teachers were rarely enthusiastic about talking to her, though. They'd always ask who the "real" mom was, as if Lana was not a genuine parent. Then they would address only Luann unless Lana directly asked them a question.

One of the most hurtful assignments for this family was the family tree. "I had to lie," says Amy. "There was no place for Lana. It was like saying my family wasn't good enough. We weren't even real. It's strange. There is a place for my grandma and aunts who we see maybe once every few years. But there's no place for Lana, my second mother, who is with me every day."

Family Trees and Other Projects

As teachers, who are we excluding without even knowing it? What assignments do we make without realizing the distress it inflicts on families? Regardless of how we feel about this issue, it's our job to ensure that these children in our classes can feel safe and thrive in our classrooms. Adding extra lines on family trees isn't very difficult, and it provides a good place to start.

Family trees can cause problems in blended families, too. Teachers need to be sensitive to their assignments to make sure they are inclusive. Unlike children in heterosexual stepfamilies, however, the child in the lesbian or gay family may never share this crucial information with you. With between one and five million lesbian mothers and one and three million gay fathers, six to fourteen million children have lesbian or gay parents in the United States today (Singer and Deschamps 1994, p. 36).

Children of various religions can feel like outsiders at times in their own classrooms. While singing holiday songs is appropriate at special times of the year like Christmas, it is difficult for children who are not Christian to sing explicitly Christian songs. There are many wonderful holiday songs that aren't explicitly religious. These are the songs that children from many religions can join in singing without guilt or conflict.

By affirming the uniqueness of each of our students, we create classroom communities where all children are able to take root and bloom. Mary Bencini has created one of these communities. Her classroom in Geneva, Illinois is a safe place for kids. Nooks and small spaces fill the room, and children sit or lay in them, reading and writing together. The bulletin boards are filled with the children's inquiry on any number or topics. On the front chalkboard one of the students has written the question, "Do you think the Bulls will win their game today?" The board is divided in half with the word "Yes" on one side, and the word "No" on the other. Magnetized pictures of each child are moved into the appropriate column as they respond to the question. Children come to the board, move their picture, and then go back to their desks. On the right side of the room, the bulletin board is completely covered, filled with the children's wondering.

One of the bulletin boards reads, "What We Are Wondering About Slaves?" The class decided as a group that they wanted to investigate slavery. Their questions filled the bulletin board. They have over forty questions about the life of slaves. It would be an impressive list for people much older than these second graders to compile.

Next, the children read many books in search of answers to their questions. Another bulletin board reads, "Can We Get A Rock From Every State?" Then each state is listed. The children wrote to all the states requesting that a rock be sent to them. As the rocks arrived, a checkmark was placed under the name of the state. Often, interesting letters accompanied the rocks, and these were shared with the class and displayed.

When I enter, the kids are busy writing and conferring. Jenny and Trina are writing a book together, as are Joe, Ron, and Don. The boys sit at a table

Jvon

my DaD Dus Not Live with me my mom end my DaD Jot Duvrst

First grade writing in response to Fly Away Home.

Inquiry

Questions Generated By Second Graders
The Underground Railroad

After reading a lot of books about the Underground Railroad, here are the questions that my second graders came up with. All questions were written on charts and then each group of four children picked five questions they wished to discuss.

We talked about what makes a good discussion question throughout the unit. They generated these questions during and after the study.

What Makes A Good Question?

It makes you think of even more questions.

It's hard to figure out.

It's something you really want to talk about.

It's challenging.

It doesn't have an easy answer.

It may not have an answer.

It doesn't always have just one answer.

You can't just look up the answer in a book.

It's sometimes interesting to talk about with others.

Questions generated by Mary Bencini's second grade class.

Questions Generated

What was it like to be a slave on a big plantation?

Why were you still a slave in the North?

Why are people so mean to others?

Did the slaves ever do anything fun?

When did slavery start?

Why was there such a thing as slavery?

Is there still slavery in some parts of the world today?

Did the white people ever have white slaves?

Did the African government try to stop slavery?

Why didn't anyone ever want sick slaves?

Who thought of starting slavery?

Why weren't slaves free when their owners died?

Why did only some owners allow their slaves to buy their freedom?

Was it better for slaves to escape in summer, winter, fall, or spring?

Why didn't black people have white people for slaves?

How could anyone ever whip a slave?

What would you do if you were a slave? Would you stay on the plantation or would you run away?

Why didn't people who were against slavery just pretend to buy slaves and then set them free?

Didn't the owners of slaves feel guilty?

What was the Fugitive Law of 1850?

If Harriet Tubman were alive, how old would she be?

How many slaves were there in all?

Were there any stations in Illinois? Were there any in Geneva?

How did they survive when they traveled on the Underground Railroad?

Why did the white people need slaves to do their work?

Why were black people used as slaves?

What was it really like to be a slave?

Why would anyone ever want to be an overseer?

Why was it against the law for a slave to learn to read and write?

Why didn't black people from Africa go to America to capture whites for slaves or to help the black slaves?

How did they keep those places such a big secret that were on the Underground Railroad?

Why did the color of your skin give you power over others?

How did the runaways keep their babies quiet?

What was it like on slave ships?

How did the slaves make medicine out of plants?

Why didn't the Presidents before Abraham Lincoln stop slavery?

Why didn't Harriet Tubman's husband help her to be free like he was?

Why did they treat black people so badly?

What were some of the secret songs?

Why do people still treat others badly just because they are different?

in the library corner, giggling and arguing about what facts they should write. Meanwhile, Dan is writing a letter to his sports hero, Michael Jordan. He can't wait until he gets a response, which he is sure will come any day.

Sara and Harold are the only boy-and-girl combination during the free choice portion of writers' workshop. There are three groups of girls and four groups of boys working together, but there is no group that has both boys and girls. I see one other boy and girl sitting at the same table, so I go over to them and ask them what they're doing. "Oh, we're not working together," Sam informs me. "We just sit at the same table."

So only Harold will work with a girl. As an outsider himself, he is the only boy who would risk such a collaboration. The other boys exclude him from their company. Harold's teacher, Mary Bencini, has supported and nurtured him throughout the school year. The most dramatic opportunity came when she encouraged his library.

Harold came to school one day and announced that he was opening his own library. He had taken all of his books and moved them onto the bookshelves he had requisitioned from his mother. Then he set to work putting library cards in each book. When that was complete, he arrived at school and announced that his library was open to the public.

Everything depended on how Mary supported him. "How wonderful!" she said. "Can I come to your library?" After school, Mary arrived at Harold's home and rang the doorbell. Harold escorted her up the stairs and into his bedroom. After carefully looking over the collection of books, she made her selection. She handed the book to Brian, the most popular boy in the class, who had volunteered to work as Harold's assistant. Brian stamped Mary's card and then told her he had to get back to work. He spent the rest of the afternoon assisting Harold with the books.

Interest continued to increase in Harold's library. Every day after school, more and more children visited his house. He had such a demand for volunteers that he had to make a schedule to keep it organized. One of Mary's friends was a member of the Geneva Library Board, and was very impressed with Harold. Representing the Library Board, she sent him a special award and a letter commending his efforts and asking if there was any way she could help him. Harold thought about it and then wrote a letter back saying that he really could use more bookshelves. He had already used up all his available space.

How might we use literacy to help outsiders become insiders? We might start like Mary, by seizing the moments that present themselves, encouraging students' projects and inquiries, and by supporting them as much as possible. A funny thing happened as Mary's class became involved in Harold's library. They began to invite him over to their houses and started to work with him by choice in the classroom. Mary believes that the other caring adults who supported Harold's library belong to a community of "those who get it." Harold's mother got it, when she allowed Harold to turn his room into a library. The library board member got it, when she took Harold's library seriously. And Mary got it, when she supported his library in as many ways as she could think of. Often, those split–second decisions we make are monumental in making a difference in kids' lives. Joining the club of "those who get it" is a great place to begin.

10 | The Inclusive Inquiry Cycle

The Authoring-inquiry Cycle provides the framework for students' literacy work. This is the foundation for using literacy to teach equity and social justice. I'm adding the word "inclusive" to highlight the issues that are involved in equity and social justice. Both girls and boys are included, as well as all historically oppressed peoples.

Inclusive Inquiry is a process in which discrimination and prejudice are fought, and a hate-free zone is created. All students pursue their questions about justice, uncovering prejudice and opening up their perceptions of other cultures. During the Inquiry Cycle, students might study other issues, but with the inclusive Inquiry Cycle, the process focuses on issues of social justice.

During the cycle, students identify potential areas for social action. We can teach kids not to settle for inequities in relationships and we can help them go into the world. Students might write letters to the local paper or the president. Students could decide that no one can say "no" when asked to play on the playground. Students might clean up a vacant lot, or agree that girls can always play kickball with the boys. Making our classrooms better places to live is just as important as improving the world. We want kids to realize that they can make a difference, and that they do.

Including all of our Questions

Teaching for Tolerance

Including All Ages

Including All Girls and Boys

Creating a Hate-Free Zone

Including All Religions

Fighting Prejudice & Discrimination

Including Reverence for the Earth

Inclusive Inquiry

Including All Families

Including Everyone in the Class

Including All Sexual Identities

Including All Girls and Boys

Including All Economic Classes

Including All Historically Oppressed People

Including All Races

Highlighting the Inclusive in Inquiry. (Henkin, 1998)

One feature of both the Inquiry and Inclusive Inquiry Cycle is the opportunity for students to learn from, and express their new understandings through, multiple literacies. Multiple literacies refers to learning from other than printed texts. When we offer multiple literacies to students, it expands both the range of expression and the number of students who can attempt to make sense of their lives. Multiple literacies require us to go beyond the written word to student expression through art, music, drama, computers, science, math, dance, gardening, etc. The list is as diverse as people's talents and interests. There are many ways that we can come to know, and each of these disciplines gives us additional ways to experience the world. Just as many of us have been afraid to really see, we've been hesitant to explore other kinds of knowing in our classrooms.

Inclusive Inquiry

Reflection

Collaborating With others

Uninterrupted Personal Engagements

Reflection

Invitations to Areas of Social Justice

Attending to Difference Tension

Uncovering Prejudice

Reflection

Discovering Potential Areas for Social Action

Opening Up our Perceptions of Other Cultures

Emphasizing the Inclusive in Inquiry. (Burke, Harste, and Short, and, in addition, Henkin, 1998)

The Multiple-Ways-of-Knowing Curriculum

Jerome Harste and Christine Leland have written about the multiple-ways-of-knowing curriculum (1990). They say that a curriculum is democratic if it provides a larger range of media to choose from, so that more students can choose a media that is meaningful to them. This diversity supports the Inquiry process. In her book, *Picture Learning Artists & Writers in the Classroom* (1994), Karen Ernst provides a vision of how art enhances literacy in her classroom. Phyllis Whitin (1996) shares examples of sketching in the inquiry cycle in her book, *Sketching Stories, Stretching Minds.* Both of these books can help classroom teachers extend opportunities for their students.

Carole Edelsky has been a mentor and an inspiration for me. She pushes us to continually go beyond our current classroom practice. Carol illuminated how critical literacy can extend our work in our classrooms. She shared the characteristics that a critical, holistic curriculum would include:

1. No or few exercises (worksheets)
2. Grounded in students' lives
3. Offers a safe place
4. Teachers share thoughts as a member of the community
5. Takes a critical stance
6. Takes a pro-justice search for voices not usually heard
7. Helps students become activists for justice and equity
   a) Helps students consider what is commonly taken for granted
   b) Helps make the world a better place

(1994)

In a critical, pro-justice classroom, we'd expand on the questions we encourage students to think about. Questions are crucial. They guide our inquiry. Both sets of questions need to be asked. The second set of questions follows the first. These are the harder questions, and often not asked in classrooms.

In Literacy Classrooms	and	In Critical, Pro-Justice, Literacy Classrooms
What do you think?		Why is it like this?
What do you notice?		Who benefits?
What are you wondering about?		Is it fair?
		What is left out?
		What isn't addressed?
What are your questions?		How can we investigate this?

Creating classroom communities that are equitable and democratic is not easy. Creating safe spaces where every voice is heard and no one is silenced is hard work. The classroom should become a place where children learn that every life is valuable and that goodness is a contribution to the world. We can't do it all in school, but it is a place to start.

The Inclusive Inquiry Cycle

Using the Inquiry Cycle, we can create pro-justice classrooms. In Inclusive Inquiry, we have a way to integrate multicultural, cross-cultural curriculum with literacy in a holistic way. In Inclusive Inquiry, we provide a framework for critical questions to arise. Rather than a multicultural unit or thematic unit, the Inclusive Inquiry Cycle provides a structure for continued implementation throughout the school year.

I've been working with teachers in developing this model over the last three years. We're calling this "Inclusive Inquiry" because we're guided by the question, "How can we create safe spaces in our classrooms where all the world's children can feel safe enough to share, and no one is silenced? There are two parts to this question. The first refers to the children in our own classroom. How can we create an atmosphere where all students can thrive? The second part involves nudging students to help expand their knowledge of all the peoples of the world, as well as to figure out how to eradicate injustice.

We've been living the Inclusive Inquiry Cycle ourselves as a two-fold process: We experience it as our students do, and we try to explore and imagine the possibilities for our classrooms. We've done much of this work in a graduate course called "Reading/Writing Relationships."

On the first night of the graduate course, I provide many invitations as we begin the Inclusive Inquiry Cycle. Invitations are just that, ideas to consider learning more about. Invitations can be in the form of books, movies, games, written or oral questions, pictures, etc. My invitations center on issues of social justice. I bring in many children's and adolescent books as well as multiple artifacts for each of the invitations. I spread the invitations around the entire room and students begin looking at the invitations as soon as they arrive on the first night. The invitations include:

1. The Holocaust
2. Strong girls and women
3. Japanese internment camps
4. World War II
5. Hispanic culture
6. African-American culture
7. Immigrants
8. Homelessness
9. Lesbian and Gay culture
10. Historically oppressed cultural and religious groups
11. Understanding of differences
12. Aging
13. Slavery
14. Outsiders

The Holocaust was the focus of one of the invitation areas in the room. The teachers entered the room to the soundtrack from *Schindler's*

List, while the movie *Shoah* was playing on the VCR. Many children's and adult books were displayed, as well as information about The Holocaust Museum in Washington, D.C. I also had art books from *The Holocaust Museum in Israel (Yad Vashem)* and Judy Chicago's and Donald Woodmans' *The Holocaust Project* (1993). I had newspapers and magazines and listings of upcoming Holocaust memorial events that were being offered in conjunction with the Holocaust Day of Remembrance. Each of the invitation areas was treated the same way, with a variety of books and artifacts.

As teachers moved around and through the areas, they had uninterrupted time to think and reflect and find their own areas of interest. I asked that they find a group to work with in which they choose one young adult or adult book of any genre and several picture books. I invited them to choose any area of social injustice and emphasized that they were free to choose any books for their literature discussions. Following that, each student would find one question to pursue and share with us in some way that included multiple literacies.

Initially, there was concern among the teachers about what they were supposed to do. Stephanie McGlynn is a fifth-grade teacher from Lake Bluff, Illinois. Stephanie describes the experience of her group in the beginning of the process.

> When it came to choosing an inquiry topic within our social justice area, my group and I experienced cognitive dissonance. This happened because we didn't really know what the professor expected. We weren't used to having freedom, but rather we were looking for some direction or structure. This is what we grew up with in school. I have done inquiry in my classroom, but I realized that I've never experienced it. We were able to bounce ideas off each other, but didn't feel confident in choosing something specific. However, all it took was a little reassurance from the professor saying we were on the right track, and we felt okay about our journey. Our inquiry experience was wonderful. We were able to take risks, experience it first–hand, and learn, all at the same time.

The literature discussions led to opportunities to collaborate and construct meaning together. Janice Besser, a teacher of adults in business, describes it this way:

> Although I have participated in literature discussions and inquiry-based learning in other classes, I have never participated to such a great ex-

tent—in both small and large group discussion. I have truly enjoyed the experience of sharing with my peers and teacher, and have both benefited and enjoyed the discussions. I enjoyed the opportunity to read both the articles and my professional book, and not have things end there. It was interesting to hear the thoughts and comments of other students as well. (I do not recall many instances in grammar school where we were asked to comment on anything we had read. Fortunately, the situation improved in my high school days.)

I found it interesting that we did not always agree, but respected and listened to the other class members. One instance in particular was the article, "Creating Minds, Created Text: Writing and Reading Relationships," written by Birnbaum and Emig. I came to the small group discussion saying how much I liked the article, and my partner said he did not like it. Neither of us changed our minds, but shared our thoughts about the article and why we felt the way we did. We discovered that we shared many of the same basic beliefs although we had differing opinions. The literature groups allowed us to share ideas, both professional and personal, as well as to gain multiple perspectives.

I found this particularly true in the situation of my professional book, *Sounds From The Heart* (Barbieri 1995). I attended an all girls high school. I have some very definite ideas as to the advantages and disadvantages of a single sex school, that I readily shared with the group. Everyone (all females) in the group really enjoyed the professional book, and certainly found its subject matter very relevant. Maureen Barbieri's recognition and admittance that she tended to favor boys in the classroom led to a wonderful story of her growth, change, and journey as a teacher. Her book was easy to read as a story. The group related on a very personal level to her comments about girls in the classroom, and came away with many wonderful techniques and ways to allow girls to be heard in the classrooms. I looked forward to reading ahead so we could continue to discuss as a group.

Barbieri's book, though read by only one group, was referred to throughout the rest of the quarter. When the group who read *Shabanu* (Staples 1989) talked about her struggle not to cave in to her culture's limited perceptions of what women could do, they related it back to the struggle of adolescent girls trying to find their voices. When one teacher reflected that we have no national holiday honoring women, we wondered what Barbieri's students might do with this insight. This intertextuality, or using a text when referring to other written or oral texts, was a characteristic of the rich literature discussions that ensued.

Janice reflects on the literature discussion and inquiry experience in this way:

It was most interesting for me to not only read about literature discussion groups and inquiry-based learning, but to participate in the processes. We were given a great deal of guidance and direction in the class, yet at the same time, we had many opportunities to select what we were interested in learning. I see that a comfortable balance can be achieved in a classroom—a balance comfortable for students as well as the teacher. You established the Inclusive Inquiry on social justice. Within that context, as students, we were able to select a social justice issue of interest to us. You provided us with books, materials, and ideas to get the group thinking.

Groups were established based on our interests, and met regularly to discuss ideas. As a group, we were then responsible for planning and presenting what we had learned about our topic. Inquiry-based learning is *not* a free-for-all as many people might think. It does not mean that students do whatever they want to do, when they want to do it. There is definite structure to the process—and I do see it as a process that does not have a definite beginning, middle, and conclusion. However, within that structure there is a great deal of room for personal choice. It is not an easy task, and requires tremendous skill and practice on the part of a teacher to be able to maintain that balance. Inquiry-based learning demands careful planning, direction, and execution on the part of the teacher. It also demands total involvement of all the participants, including the teacher.

I thoroughly enjoyed all aspects of the class. We did not sit for hours and listen to lectures about educational theories and practice. We discussed different theories and approaches to learning, and then tried them ourselves. How else can we learn how to become better teachers? Why should we expect anything different of our students?

Chris Poziemski, a teacher at Harper Community College, describes her investigation into her personal inquiry project:

I was interested in more topics than I could pursue during the ten-week class. I was thinking, "Oh darn, I can only read one of these novels. And I'd like to do strong women, and gays, and the holocaust." On several occasions, I stopped to peruse the young adult shelves at Borders and purchased several extra professional books to look over this summer. This is exactly what we want to happen in our classes. We want to hook our students and let them run with their interests. We want classroom life to impact daily life.

It was also fun to do the topic search on what turned out to be women's rights in Pakistan. I did some "wandering and wondering." I wasn't quite sure what I wanted to know and I worked for hours looking at documents by Muslim men about women in the Koran, by Amnesty International on human rights violations in Pakistan, and by book critics who had included *Shabanu* on their lists of recommended books for adolescents. I actually didn't know what my question was right away, which was an interesting discovery. I liked that I didn't have to cover a topic and report exhaustively, but was allowed to explore the topic from a diverse perspective, an aspect of inquiry mentioned by Short and Harste in *Creating Classrooms for Authors and Inquirers*.

Chris's project ended up focusing on polygamy, a reality in Shabanu's world. She found information, particularly on the World Wide Web, about the pros and cons of polygamy. She had never thought there might be advantages, and this opened up new inquiries. Chris's description of how she got to her question is important. With children too, time and experiences are necessary before we know what our burning question will be. If we rush the process, we may never be as engaged as we might have been. As Chris attended to the difference between her perception of polygamy and the way some cultures view reality, she was responding to the tension between two realities. As she read about some of the positive aspects of polygamy, she was forced to confront her own prejudices and the tension between conflicting versions of the truth, just like Sarah, Areila, and Sue were forced to do in their sixth–grade study of the Crusaders. As Chris thought about the idea that, in polygamy, people are less likely to get lonely, and women can have careers and still have someone home to take care of the kids, she too had to consider life from another view.

This is the beginning of inclusive inquiry, the merging of the inquiry cycle with teaching social justice. By using a foundation of multicultural and cross-cultural education, we're bringing it into the literacy curriculum. By incorporating a critical perspective, we're emphasizing the action part of social action. Christine Bennett (1995) emphasizes four core values in multicultural education that lead to six goals for implementation. They are:

Core Values for Multicultural Education
1. Acceptance and appreciation of cultural diversity
2. Universal human rights
3. Responsibility to the world community and
4. Reverence for the Earth

Goals for Implementation
1. Multiple historical perspectives
2. Strengthen cultural consciousness
3. Strengthen intercultural competence
4. Combat racism, sexism, and other forms of prejudice and discrimination
5. Increase awareness of the state of the planet and global dynamics
6. Build social action skills

These goals and core values provide a firm foundation for teaching social justice. How can they be implemented in classrooms? In this model, it is assumed that the teacher is making all the decisions. The teacher does the planning and decides what the students are going to study and how. Although multicultural textbooks emphasize that this shouldn't be a one-shot activity or a single project, that isn't how it is usually carried out. And though they emphasize structural change in the curriculum, most teachers who incorporate multicultural goals do it through projects they've designed.

Inclusive Inquiry offers us a deep and authentic way to incorporate a multicultural curriculum. The teacher will still make decisions about curriculum through the invitations she will offer her students. I chose the umbrella of social justice, but within that umbrella, students had opportunities to pursue their own questions. The books I offered as invitations were critical. The Appendix at the end of this book lists books that have worked for me and many of the teachers with whom I've worked. This is by no means an exhaustive list, and I'd love to hear about your favorite selections.

Through the individual and group inquiry, conflicting ideas are raised. Because reflection is an ongoing part of the cycle, these ideas are studied. In Chris's case, this served as the beginning for understanding another culture. This is an authentic way to engage students and to bring about real change. Inquiry provides the vehicle for multicultural work to be realized. By adding critical literacy, we provide the critique we need as we uncover prejudices and inconsistencies. The question "Whose interest is served?" can lead to the first steps of social action. When we are encouraging children to think about "In whose interest is it that we study what we study?", it should be within the context of children having some voice in following the issues that they identify. Inclusion means the inclusion of all voices, especially those that have been historically oppressed and therefore silenced. All the voices and interests of the students in our rooms should be included.

Sharing what was learned offers another powerful opportunity for students to think about other issues and cultures besides the one they are working on. Often, it is the variety of the ways they experience the presentations that helps them to construct meaning. Tim Holly, a preschool teacher with the Chicago public schools; and Janice Besser, a teacher of adults, studied homelessness. In their presentation, they constructed varied scenarios that might lead to families becoming homeless. They passed out slips of paper containing the scenarios to small groups in our classroom and had us role-play the situations and then problem-solve possible alternatives for them. One scenario was a battered wife, another was a mentally ill person. Where could they go? How could they survive? The strong women group had us participate in a choral reading from *Shabanu*. After sharing facts about slavery, we were asked to express the injustice through watercolors or clay. The outsider group had us interpret a short story through musical instruments. These examples of transmediation, or interpreting meaning through other sign systems (in these cases, drama, choral reading, art and music) helped us to understand these issues and cultures in a deeper way. Short and Harste believe that you can't separate transmediation in multiple sign systems from the Inquiry Cycle. I agree, and in this same way, you can't separate teaching for social justice from the Inquiry Cycle. I am also using the term Inclusive Inquiry to remind us of the inclusive interrelationships involved.

Tim describes the Inclusive Inquiry process as he experienced it for himself:

> Generating the questions seemed to be the easy part. There was relatively little that I knew about homelessness other than it was a social issue that would not go away, even in the best of economic times. Finding sources of information wasn't difficult, but finding quality children's books proved to be more of a challenge. Reading a young adult novel gave us a chance to relate what we were reading to what we were writing. Although the book ends on a note of optimism, it is open ended enough to generate more questions. That is where reflection came in. We did not attempt to solve the issue of homelessness. What we could do was to look at the issues involved and attempt to find a creative response that would benefit all those effected by the social injustice created by homelessness.

Having a chance to discuss issues related to the topic of homelessness was an aid to reflection. It was a way to exchange ideas and interpretations. It lead to new ideas and a better understanding of the consequences of a failed social policy. I think sensitive issues like homelessness, child abuse, substance abuse, violence, and any other social problem that confronts us today can be presented to students through inquiry. Inquiry can also be used across the curriculum to help students construct their own learning.

The Holocaust group had read *The Devil's Arithmetic* (Yolen 1988) as one of their choices for literature discussion. The book begins with the Jewish Passover service and dinner that takes place in the home. We were all invited to sit around the beautiful, white lace tablecloth that was placed on the floor of the classroom. Two candles were lit and the service began. We made and ate the sandwich made of matzo, bitter herbs, and chloroses—a combination of apples, nuts, and wine. We each had a small paper cup of wine and had begun feeling relaxed when four members rushed into the room and started screaming at us. "Hurry up. Get up now. You have no time to pack. You're going to the work camp."

They shouted and screamed at us and I felt myself panicking. I knew this wasn't real, but I was terrified. I moved out of the tiny space my group was cramped in and was screamed at again. At least it felt like screaming, but I don't think she really raised her voice very much. "Over there," she said. I was given a number on cellophane tape and it was slapped on my arm. "You may not remove it."

We were ushered back into the classroom and told to go in a corner. The names of concentration camps surrounded the room. I was in Auschwitz, and when I realized it, I felt my blood go cold. I was terrified. After a few more minutes of feeling alone, lost, and terrified, we were brought together and asked to debrief our experience. Then the Holocaust group shared more of their research. One person investigated the concentration camps, while another had wanted to know the significance of the tattooed numbers of each prisoner. The third student researched the reasons people hate each other, to try to understand how the Holocaust could have occurred. We listened to their research attentively.

I've read many books about the Holocaust and visited many exhibits about it. But I experienced the Holocaust in an entirely new and different way that day, with an understanding of the terror that has never left me. I left my cellophane number on my arm until it fell off several days later.

Julie Triner sums up Inclusive Inquiry and the potential for social action in this way:

Teaching for social justice was something I did not quite grasp until I took this course. I have been searching for ways to make students' learning more meaningful and motivating to them. Topics of interest to sixth graders, I thought, were not always the most in-depth subjects. My students do not have a clue as to what happens in the world. They are oblivious to what happens outside their own little worlds and outside of our community. The wonderful novels and picture books that have been written about gangs, violence, homelessness, understanding differences, aging, and death are designed to bring a world of understanding to them. The text sets that address these issues provide students with a wealth of awareness that they otherwise would not have.

Not only do they present facts and scenarios, but they also provide insight to the thoughts and feelings of people who have experienced life in such a different way. The new perspectives that these voices have to share are so beneficial to others. Even though we aren't in the habit of teaching values education, we can teach students to appreciate what they have. Exposing them to the experiences of others and encouraging them to get involved is enough. They will make up their own minds about how to get involved.

11 | Using Literacy to Create Social Justice Classrooms

Dealing with Death and Homelessness

Mickey Nuccio cares deeply about her students. "Sometimes I think my students are the real outsiders in life." When I ask her what she means, she elaborates. "It's just that we're in this run–down school in a poor inner-city neighborhood in Chicago. We're not a magnet school and our parents don't have any power. The paint is peeling on the walls, and there's a general feeling of indifference to the plight of the children."

Life in Mickey's classroom, though, is anything but grim. The walls are filled with the children's brightly colored artwork and their stories. The baby ducks have hatched, and their inquiry about ducks fills every available space. Many of the children are writing and illustrating non-fiction books about ducks. Books fill the room, but even more importantly, there is a feeling of happiness and well-being when you walk through the door. Children are constantly talking, reading, and writing. They discuss important issues whenever they come up. If there is a problem, the first graders deal with it.

Mickey uses literature as a path into the children's lives. Whenever the world gets too difficult to handle, the class turns to stories to help them find their way. When a second grader was murdered after school hours, the children were devastated. While special counseling teams composed of community psychiatrists and social workers would have descended on a suburban school, no such help was available for Mickey's students. The principal of the school visited Mickey's class and said that Teddy, a fourth grader, had been killed in a fire. Mickey's class was the only one that asked her any questions.

"Why did Teddy die?" Hulio wanted to know.

"It was just one of those things," replied the principal.

"How did he die?"

"He was killed."

"Where did he go?" the children asked.

"He's in heaven now."

The principal left and that was the sum total of the grief counseling provided by the school system. Even though it wasn't discussed in school, some of the children knew. The next day the kids started talking about Teddy.

"I had a scary dream. I dreamed Teddy had come back."

Mickey asked the class if they'd like to talk about their dreams. Everyone was eager to share.

"I had a good feeling. I dreamed about my dad after he died."

Dream sharing became very popular for the next week. The students would arrive at school and start sharing immediately. Mickey asked them if they might want to draw and write about their dreams, and soon dream pictures began emerging. Many of them had fires prominently displayed. Leroi asked Mickey if she had ever been in a fire. Mickey replied that she had not, then asked Leroi if he had.

"I was in a fire," Leroi stated matter-of-factly.

"What happened?" Mickey asked softly.

"My baby brother died."

The class had been listening intently. Now, many students began to speak up.

"I was in a fire."

"Me, too. My mommy died."

"My house was burned. We had to go to a shelter."

"What I learned," Mickey recalls later, "Was that I was the only one in my classroom whose life hadn't been touched by fire. My students thought fire was normal. They were surprised I didn't share their experience. The really scary thing is that I almost didn't find this out. I don't know why I asked Leroi if he had been in a fire. I really didn't think he had. I almost missed finding out something profoundly important about the lives of my students."

I   Love   my   big sister
and   my   mother   and my
father
I love   my sister
I   Was   crying but my mother
Love   my   sister   and my
frther   Love   my   sister but my
sister   Was   beding and I wasfell

Sharing our lives.

The children continued to share their dreams, which often focused on fire and their fears. They had time to talk about these dreams, and write about and draw them. Mickey decided to share *Badger's Parting Gifts* with them. In the book, Badger knows that he will soon go through the long tunnel in the sky (he knows he will soon die). He is ready for the journey. His only regret will be leaving his friends. Even though he tries to prepare them, they are not ready for the loss. Badger's friends spend the winter remembering him and the joy he brought into their lives. When spring comes, they are able to remember him with joy and appreciation. The children immediately started talking about death.

"Why did Timmy have to die?" they asked.

"Because he was murdered."

"Why did someone hurt him?"

"Because sometimes adults are mean to kids."

"I didn't know what to say," Mickey told me. "These are babies. They are only first graders."

Mickey watched her kids carefully. Their writing during the next few days showed an understanding of death. Brothers and sisters had died. Babies had died. Grandparents and friends had died. Mom's boyfriend had died. Several of the children drew pictures of people holding guns in their dying scenes.

"I learned that I might not like it, but it really is my students' reality, said Mickey. "The kids wanted to talk about the issues. It makes me sad to think about how few teachers allow it to happen."

The children started talking about the shelter in the neighborhood, which led Mickey to share *Fly Away Home*. In this book, a young boy and his dad try to survive by living at the airport. To be able to do this, they have to blend in as much as possible or risk being evicted from the airport. Although the father doesn't have enough money to rent an apartment, he is able to save money while he works. They wash in the restroom, and try to look as presentable as possible. The students listened carefully as Mickey read the story.

"Why does he live in an airport?" they wanted to know. This was a different experience for them.

"Yeah, why doesn't he go to the shelter?" Several of the kids asked. They knew about shelters.

"How come he had to worry about being put out?"

"How come he had to try not to be noticed?"

"If he was my friend, I would have helped him," said Edwin.

"Yeah. In the book, when the other family found a home, they could have shared it with them," Teresa said.

The students showed great empathy and sophistication when writing about homelessness. Several of the children wrote about their own experiences of being homeless or knowing someone who is homeless. Talking about the issue, reading about it, and having abundant opportunities for continued reflection, writing, and reading is important in even first grade. Mickey could have avoided these topics because they made her feel uncomfortable. By bringing social issues into first-grade classrooms, we're making powerful statements. We're saying that we hear our students. We know that they must deal with these difficult events. We care about them and it is good to speak their truth. Literacy truly becomes a vehicle that means something. Through literacy, we're all affirmed, supported, and able to find our way.

Discussing Violence

I was reading *Just One Flick of a Finger* by Marybeth Lorbiecki to Geri Socha's sixth–grade class at Columbus School in Cicero. This story, told in poetry and rap, showed how one boy got tired of being picked on, "borrowed his father's gun, and accidentally shot his best friend." The students listened attentively to the text and immediately began their literature discussions. I looked across the sea of students, most wearing the blue-and-white school uniforms. The hum of kids speaking in Spanish and English filled the room. The kids were animated as they argued the merits of the story.

"He never should have stole his dad's gun."

"But he had to have protection."

"That's the wrong kind of protection."

"Maybe, but I'd do the same. I don't want to be the only one who doesn't have a gun."

As Geri and I circulated among the groups, it became increasing clear that the kids knew what they were talking about. They were arguing personally. "How many of you have been with someone who has had a gun?" Geri asked. Everyone's hand went up. We looked at each other. "How many of you have been shot at?" Twelve of the twenty-four students raised their hands.

"It's definitely in their lives," said Pat Pavlich. "There was a drive-By shooting in the back of our school this year. It happened just as the kids were being dismissed. That's why I decided to bring in books like *Drive-By*

Heysha Martinez   102
Jan. 31, 1997
Language Arts

Abraham

At Warren Park School, there is a bright and wonderful student in sixth grade named Abraham, but he is at the bottom of the pecking-order. I was there when he wanted to jump rope, instead, they pushed him and started to call him names. I also overheard that the boys were at the front of their #103 line, but didn't let Abraham stand by them because they think he is a girl.

Nicole Bosi is like a best friend to Abraham. She is kind to him and always defends him from the bullies.

I think he has changed a bit, but is turning back to how he was. Room #103 tells him not to talk to us because they don't want Abraham to have friends that care about him.

Working to include everyone.

I think what is going to happen in the future is something awful. He would probably turn into Ken A., Chris M., and Ricky L. because he says he wants to be cool, too.

I think this problem has changed my life. I've learned an enormous lesson from Abraham and the kids in room #103. I've learned that you shouldn't be a bully to anyone because it truly hurts their feelings.

by Lynne Ewing and *Just One Flick of a Finger*. After my class read *Drive-By*, the kids didn't want to discuss it. They thought it was a true story. One of my students' shared that her cousin was killed this year. Shootings occur here and they occur in Mexico. When the kids discussed this book, they shared their own life experiences. They've run for cover when kids have pulled out guns. They've been approached to join gangs. Fortunately, many of them have strong, loving families. They work at keeping their children out of harm's way. The kids are told to go straight home after school. Many of the mothers pick them up after school. These kids have many wonderful gifts in their lives. They have lots of things to be thankful for."

Pat believes that literature opens the door to an abundance of conversations. "We do lots of talking, lots of reading, and lots of writing. We're constantly trying to problem-solve. We talk about how important it is to do something for equity and justice. When there is conflict on the playground and in the classroom, we try to get through the hot-headedness. We do a lot of conflict resolution. We work at solving problems without resorting to violence. We're constantly writing about how to say 'No.' We look for new ways to approach problems, and we try to figure out how to have more loyalty to our own families than to gangs."

The students in Pat Pavlich's class gain strength in numbers in their search for justice. They learn to stand up against the bullies. "I really see this as the pay-off for teaching for justice, " says Pat. "Doing something doesn't mean you have to do something in the world. Doing something right here in our school is important. Learning to face injustice and live democratically in our classroom is a major accomplishment. Every child who solves problems through words rather than guns represents victory. In a class where friendships are cherished and bullies confronted, social justice thrives."

Home-School Connections: Contact Logs, Family Math, After-School Clubs

Warren Park School in Cicero set out to make as many home-school connections as possible. Because it is a poor school, it applied for and received a series of grants that helped it initiate and carry out the project. The staff wanted to recruit families and make them feel welcome. Shelly Irwin-Negron, the principal, began "Coffee and Conversations," where parents could visit the school and chat with the teachers and the principal. As the faculty and the parents brainstormed, they decided to work together in educating the students about the Hispanic culture through feasts and food. Teachers visited students' homes and parents visited classrooms in preparation for the project. Contact logs were used whenever parents and teachers made connections. This was a notebook in which every person recorded the hours spent on a project, and what the project was. In this way, they were able to document all the work.

Family Math was one of the projects that became quite successful. Family Math consisted of concrete projects that parents could do to help advance their children's math understandings. Parents volunteered for the training to become leaders. They led workshops for parents after school and in the evening. The teachers attended these workshops, so in essence were taught by the parents. This was the kind of reciprocal relationship that Luis Moll talks about. It was the parents who taught the teachers, and the teachers who were the learners. Having the teachers ask questions of the parents made it easier for the parents to do the same.

The grants also allowed the teachers and parents to plan an exciting after-school learning experience. They offered opportunities for tutoring, ways to support achievement, and interesting educational experiences that both students and parents could participate in. They reinforced home, school, and community relationships. All teachers and many parents were involved as the project was initiated. One club was called *Headliners*. This school-wide newspaper was designed to promote reading and writing. Students and parents wrote articles about school events. Both the English and Spanish local newspapers promised to help with *Headliners*. Bob Lifka of *The Cicero Life* newspaper led workshops for students and parents.

The after–school clubs were offered so that students could belong to two clubs per session. The choices included:

Adventures in Art	Book-making
Headliners	Improvisation
Dance	Band
Chorus	Computer Lab with Internet Hook-up
Storytelling	Parent Support Group
Literature Circles	Learning English for Adults

The clubs continued throughout the year at full enrollment. This was especially amazing because all the children were bussed to Warren Park from other schools in the district. Some traveled a distance, but were able to make plans to stay after school. Most of the classes in this middle grade school are bilingual. The school made this a strength to draw upon.

Peer Mediation

Another successful program was Peer Mediation, begun several years ago in the school. The students participated in an eight-session training program voluntarily after school. During lunch and recesses, these students arbitrated all conflict on the playground. They made use of discussion, reflection, and writing when resolving disputes. The principal met with them once a month to review procedures, share strategies used during the month, and brainstorm potential issues.

A feeling of peace and happiness now reverberates throughout Warren Park school. Students are constantly greeting and hugging the teachers and the principal, Shelly. They are used to feeling comfortable in school and in charge of their lives and their school. So, when Carol Ramark's sixth–grade class noticed that a new little boy was being ostracized and excluded, they brought their concerns to their teacher.

"What do you think we can do about it?" Carol asked her class.

"Let's write about it," was the response. "Maybe we'll get some good ideas."

Carol describes what happened next:

The actual heartbreaking agony this boy endures each day was not evident in my students' writing. (This is interesting, too; perhaps they're too young to hurt or empathize so deeply. Perhaps having to *write* their feelings was the stumbling block. Perhaps the uniqueness of the writing topics for students with limited English vocabulary was the problem.)

In November when we spoke about "kids on the outside," I thought about Abraham instantly. At first glance he doesn't look too different from the others, but he's very intelligent, quiet, talks softly, wears thicker-than-usual glasses and seems kindly, which may equate with effeminate to the very rough and tumble macho male leaders in that class. I think his background is Middle Eastern. He doesn't defend himself, so both boys and girls in his class have a field day with making fun of him, pushing him, calling him names, and laughing at him.

The challenge for my class was to not let the other class know we're interested or even aware of Abraham. I don't believe any student has given away the secret. We said it would only make him feel worse if he knew he was our "project." Secondly, we would try to befriend him—take his side sometimes, talk with him or ask him to join in a game occasionally, maybe walk home with him some afternoons. My class is a more gentle group, a bit more sensitive, and took this project seriously. It fit with our sense of social justice. They wanted to do something, but as individuals were shy about standing up to some of the very large, intimidating leaders in the other class. The strength in numbers concept worked for my class. They could finally stand up to the boys who were the ring-leaders as well as the mean-spirited girls in the other class.

I am convinced my current students have experienced a situation that has made them more mature. They will probably not be quite as mean as they would have been otherwise. By thinking about injustice, we acted upon an ugly situation at our school. Everyone just looked the other way. For the rest of this year, however, one totally unhappy little boy will experience some peer friendship and camaraderie he would otherwise not have had.

Creating Student Heroes at Burnham School

Peggy Nadziejko's fifth–grade classroom has been transformed into a time machine. The magnificent structure stands in a corner, but the whole room shows signs of time traveling. The students divide into small groups, choosing the decade in the 20th century they found most interesting. Together, each member of the research team discovers key events of the decade. They look into world affairs, wars and revolts, people, and events. Banners conveying their discoveries and artwork decorate the walls.

There is much to see in this classroom. Color and shapes caress your eyes in every direction. Balloons, hanging children's art, students' books and many, many books of all genres sit in baskets and spread across the ceiling. Inspirational sayings such as "Dance With Life" and "Leave a Brilliant Light Behind," are posted throughout the room. That's what Peggy does with her students.

Sue Sparks, an ESL teacher at Burnham, explains Peggy's magic. "She really cares about her students. She cares about human beings. Our school is gigantic. We have over 1300 students. Even teachers can get lost in the crowd. But Peggy truly cares about people. Each year she introduces herself to the new teachers and offers to help them in any way she can. She checks in with them. She is such a good friend."

Peggy's students know that she cares about them. She hugs them every day. She inspires them and encourages them. She believes in the potential of every child. That's why it was especially discouraging when Erick got shot. He became a hero in her classroom.

The story of Erick's shooting was fuzzy. He and some of his friends were in the backyard looking at a gun when his friend pointed it at him and shot him. They didn't think it was loaded. Before the shooting, Erick was ignored by many of the older gang members, but now everyone congratulates him. In the classroom, too, he was respected. Erick had been shot. Erick was a hero.

"I couldn't believe it," Peggy said. "I wanted my class to see what real heroes and heroines are. I wanted them to know that you have to give of yourself and care about others." Peggy and her students designed a service project together. They brainstormed ideas about how they could help each of their families, neighborhood, and their communities. They developed a list of 60 possible ways that they could make a difference in someone else's life. The ideas generated were:

1. Visiting a senior citizen living alone
2. Going out to lunch with someone lonely
3. Making food baskets for the homeless
4. Playing bingo at the nursing home
5. Doing things around the house without being asked
6. Helping to snow off the car
7. Babysitting

8. Cleaning a bathroom
9. Helping people younger than yourself
10. Cleaning backyards
11. Helping senior citizens that need help
12. Going to the store for someone
13. Washing cars
14. Carrying bags for people
15. Washing clothes
16. Walking dogs
17. Taking out the garbage
18. Talking to someone
19. Listening to someone
20. Bringing food or clothes to a shelter
21. Offering to help out the shelter
22. Going to the nursing home and singing songs
23. Shoveling snow
24. Cleaning someone's porch
25. Cleaning up blocks and parks
26. Being a good role model
27. Playing chess or checkers with someone who is lonely
28. Taking someone to a game
29. Cleaning a garage
30. Visiting a sick person
31. Helping someone (i.e. give someone an umbrella)
32. Mopping floors
33. Giving/donating clothes
34. Sweeping streets
35. Setting the table
36. Washing dishes
37. Planting flowers
38. Giving cards on holidays
39. Repairing something
40. Taking a person for a walk
41. Recycling
42. Helping someone if they get hurt
43. Cooking
44. Going to work and volunteering
45. Sharing
46. Washing windows

47. Playing with little kids and setting a good example
48. Cleaning up the classroom
49. Playing a game with someone
50. Cutting weeds
51. Cleaning house
52. Raking leaves
53. Teaching people self-defense
54. Giving tune-ups
55. Watering plants
56. Making people happy who are sad
57. Helping to carry books
58. Feeding pets
59. Adopting a block and helping to clean it up
60. Volunteering to help out if someone doesn't do the job

Next they decided how many hours to work and developed the purpose of the project. They decided they should work on the project for a month, and that everyone should do at least ten hours of work. When students expressed an interest in doing more, they developed a scheme where extra hours counted for more credit. They all agreed that twenty-one hours of service would be exceptional but attainable. They developed a form by which adults could verify their work.

Developing the purpose of the project took some time. They finally decided and put their ideas on the following poster:

Why are we doing this?
to help people
leave a brilliant light behind
to make people happy
to learn responsibility
have fun
to get a good grade

The class designed rules that were relevant to the project. The children acknowledged that safety was important. They decided they couldn't accept money, they couldn't be rude, and that it was important to be polite. They also decided to get parental permission and never to go into anyone's house without it. The children would report each day on how their work was going.

Howard sits at his table with Jose, Juan, and Teresa. His blond hair is cut close. As he eagerly raises his hand, his tummy sticks out from his shirt,

Serive	Hours	Signature	Date	comments
Nursing home	1 hr		may	I really liked it
Trash	14 hr		April	It was hard
Dishes	84 hr		April	I don't like it
Clean yard	8 hr		April	Tarable
Nursing Home	3:30		April	I ♡'ed it
Nursing Home	4:30		April	I ♡ed it
Nursing Home	5:30		April	I ♡ed it
Nursing Home	3 hr		April	I ♡ed it
Borad metting	2 hr		April	It was ok
A. Rose	2 hr		April	I like it alot
Trash	14 hr		2 weeks	It was hard
Dog walk	14 hr		2 weeks	It was ok
Clean dises	14 hr		April	I hated it!
Juana	1 hr		Mad	It was cool)
Nursing Home	20 min		Weekend	I ♡'ed it
Nursing Home	1 hr		Weekend	I ♡ed it
Bath Baby	30 min		Weekend	It was mess
Bath Baby	30 min		Weekend	It was mes
Trash	14 hr		2 weeks	It was hard
Dog	14 hr		2 weeks	It was ok
Clean Anuts home	8 hr		2 weeks	It was so so
Clean room	2 hr		may	I hated it
Nursing Home	3 hr		may	I ♡'ed it
Nursing Home	2:30		may	I ♡'ed it
Clean room	1 hr		may	I hated it
By:				
Sarah				
Norman				

Record of service hours.

and he keeps pulling it down, hoping to keep himself covered. He listens attentively as Maria tells of babysitting and Edwin relates that he picked garbage off the street as he was taking care of the block. He grins as he relates his project.

"I spent Friday after school at the nursing home with Jose and Teresa. Then we went back all day on Saturday and Sunday, and I went after school on Monday, too."

Peggy shakes her head in astonishment. "Where did you go? How did you get in? Who did you work with? What did they do when you came back so much?"

Howard's smile spreads across his face. "We went to the same one you took us to. We went to find our special friends. You know, the ones we spent time with in December."

"But that was so far away," Peggy says. "How did you get there?"

"Our parents," Jose chimes in. "We bugged them until one of them drove us each day."

"At first we had to explain why we were there," adds Maria.

"But not anymore," says Howard as the other two shook their heads in agreement. "Now they see us and they just buzz us in. They don't get anyone to accompany us or anything."

During this conversation, Erick listened intently. He had been quiet as the children shared their projects. Howard, Juan, and Maria were the heroes and heroines of the moment.

"What do you do with them?" asks Peggy.

"Lots of things," says Howard. "We play games, but mostly we sit and talk. They like to see us, and we like to go there."

Howard, Jose, and Maria are learning what is important. They are encouraged to think and to act ethically. They are learning that they can make a difference. "It's literacy that supports my students' efforts in the world," says Peggy. Through reading and writing, they can deal with the world. Because my kids are researchers, they know how to attack a problem. They believe there isn't any problem too great for them to find a solution to. I think they just might be right!"

Debbie Schreiner teaches fifth grade in Geneva, Illinois. During a conversation with Peggy, she wondered how she might involve her students in a similar project. "They have no clue what it's like to give of yourself. I don't want a project where they bring in money or goods. That doesn't really touch them."

As Debbie and Peggy continued talking, they tried to imagine the first step. "When I think about it," says Peggy, "my whole class was set up to do this from the beginning of the year. We began by visiting places that need us, like the homeless shelter and the animal shelter. We put on a show for the nursing home." Peggy's class made a lot of initial visits, in which they learned about the problems of their community.

There was also a constant emphasis on caring about others. They visited the mayor of Cicero, who became a friend they could rely on. They called her with problems and she responded each time. Recently, when the mayor was under stress with difficult problems, they went to her office with a gift and kind words. They put their arms around her and told her not to give up. "Whatever her political problems," said Peggy, "they wanted her to know she had made a difference in their lives." By the time the service projects began, the kids felt comfortable visiting several community organizations and the nursing home on their own.

Peggy was awarded the Golden Apple, an honor for teachers. Ten teachers in Illinois each year were chosen out of the hundreds who were nominated. In conjunction with the award, the local public television station filmed her classroom. They wanted to visit the nursing home, and so the whole class brought the film crew to the place where they now felt so at home. Howard, Juan, and Maria carefully orchestrated the event. They made sure that Mrs. Karcz was filmed in her wheelchair. Both boys helped their friend, Mr. Nun, get into the film. Since Mr. Nun had trouble walking, he missed most of the filming. The boys ran to his room, and, each at his side, shouted to the film crew to wait until Mr. Nun reached them. Mr. Nun was filmed with Howard and Juan at his side.

"These are my grandchildren," Mrs. Karcz told the photographers. "My own children live too far away and hardly ever come. I don't know why these kids care about me, but they do. They come all the time. These are my real grandchildren." By the time the film crew left, they all had tears in their eyes. "I'm going home and calling my mother," one of the crew told Peggy.

A High Tea was planned to thank all the people who had worked with Peggy's children. The children made scones and finger sandwiches and, of course, tea. They invited all of the women they had interviewed and their friends from the nursing home. Maria worried about how Mrs. Karcz could attend because she was in a wheelchair. Her father offered to use the family's van to go get her. Mrs. Karcz was thrilled. She went to the nursing home beauty shop and had her hair permed. She put on a pretty dress and sat waiting. Mrs. Karcz waited and waited until she was finally informed that the nursing home would not allow Maria's dad to drive her. Neither his van nor the school had ramps that were wheelchair accessible.

Peggy's class lived the inclusive inquiry cycle. Their previous experiences have led to new questions about equity and fairness—in this case, for an older friend who was confined to a wheelchair. The kids felt heartbroken for Mrs. Karcz. This was so unfair. They imagined her just sitting there and waiting for them. Mrs. Karcz never made it to the party. Then they got angry. Why was life so unfair? This was one of the crucial moments. Their anger could have easily turned to despair and hopelessness. "Let's tell the mayor," said Howard. The class agreed. They felt empowered and knew they could make a difference. They sat down and wrote letters explaining the problems caused by the lack of wheelchair accessibility and asked what steps could be taken to fix the situation. Their inquiry led them to other problems people in wheelchairs face in their lives. They also started investigating other buildings in the community that were lacking ramps. "Because my kids are researchers, they have the tools to solve problems," says Peggy. "They also have the self-confidence to know they can make a difference."

That's what Debbie wants for her students, too. Peggy suggests that they start by identifying the needs in their own community. "Is there a Meals on Wheels program? Do the local churches and synagogues give shelter to the homeless?" Debbie asks if there is a way that Peggy's class could advise her class. They brainstorm ideas like pen pals, the Internet, and joint field trips. The power of these suggestions is that Peggy's class will serve as advisors to the others. This isn't a project where the affluent children are helping others. This is a project where everyone is working to make others' lives in their communities a little bit better.

"That's really what it is all about," says Dave Domonic, principal of Peck School in Chicago. "I tell our students that no one is going to remember you for what you owned. The only thing that matters is if you tried to make someone else's life a little bit nicer. I'm proud that our school is racially mixed and that I live in a racially mixed neighborhood. The only way to break down the barriers of prejudice and suspicion is for us to live and work together. We all want the same things. We want the opportunity to live happy and safe lives. We want to live in peace. And if we're lucky, we want to be able to make a difference in other people's lives." This is what we need to teach our children.

My experience

One day when my teacher said that we had to do service projects, Me and my friend Jimmy went to the nursing home. Then we visited the nursing home again and the third time we brought another friend, sarah. Then, from that day on, we went to the nursing home every day. We meet lot's of people there. We Read them books, Played with them, and Some times made them fell better when they were felling down. We go and talk to our friends in the nursing home. There names our Louis, Thomas, Maira, Grace, Francies, Hidy, Carnella, Daisy, Jean, andy, and Lilian our aerobics teacher for the nursing home. They are one of our best friends there. It's fun because we feel good about our selfs.

We feel like if we have a halo over us. and when we leave we are very glad to do this. Mrs. Nadzie" so inspired us to do what we are doing. I think my friends and me make a diffrence, and also my teacher. It's one of the best thing there is. To help people, and that's what were there for.

Describing the service project experience.

12 | What If My Class Is Not Diverse?

What if my class is not diverse? Is that even possible? Maybe what we mean is that we teach in an affluent area, or that our kids are all mostly the same race or religion. Perhaps what we mean is that our students perceive themselves as being alike. So how do we build awareness and appreciation for different cultures in this situation?

The reality is that every classroom has diversity, and this fact is getting more difficult to deny. With the inclusion of special-education students and the increasing diversity of cultures in America, it's hard to find a classroom in which everyone is alike. "It starts with building classroom community, " says Debbie Gurvitz. "We always celebrate each other." Debbie is a kindergarten teacher in Glenview, Illinois. Her classroom is a composite of talk, energy, and projects. She works hard to promote friendship among all her students. There are no assigned seats and every girl is paired with a boy buddy to accomplish the work in their class.

Promoting Tolerance

There can be hidden varieties of diversity in a community. For Debbie's school, it is social class. There is a low-income trailer park in the area, and these children often feel left out. Debbie works to create positive self-esteem for every child. "I tell my kids that we are all worthy." There are difficult problems that her children face. One child's mother left three months ago. Another was abandoned by her dad. A third child's sister is going through chemotherapy for a blood disorder. Another child's father is in jail and several of the children have physical disabilities.

"I need to be tolerant, and my tolerance has spread to my students. No one has a best friend, because we're all each others' friends. We need to tolerate our differences as well as respect them." Debbie never separates the children by sexes. "We have one line. I vary how the children line up. Maybe one day I'll call them by the colors they have on. On another day we'll line up by hot or cold lunch." Debbie watches her students carefully to make sure they are working together equally and that she is calling on them fairly. "I watch a lot. I ask myself if I am looking at a situation with equity."

Debbie tries to involve her kindergartners in projects that benefit others. "Every month we give to someone else. We recycle our school supplies by donating them to a homeless shelter. We've donated to hospitals. We had a book drive to replace the books that were lost when a school in the city lost their books in a fire. I want my kids to truly understand that its good to receive and not always to get."

The close classroom community that Debbie has fostered pays off in many ways. "There are always kids who bug each other," she says, but her students have learned to talk through their problems and resolve conflicts as they arise. "I heard one of my boys tell another that he needed to talk to him because he was getting ready to be angry with him. I felt so proud that they were able to work out the conflict with words."

Multicultural teaching is important for everyone. "My children live in the world. I want them to respect differences. They need to know that we're more alike than different," Debbie says. She talks about gay and lesbian families with her young children so they won't be afraid and spread inaccuracies. "It's not traditional, so kids need to understand that there are all different kinds of ways to have families. There's no point telling those families to go back in the closet. I want kids to know it's not anything to be afraid of." Whether it's alternative families or people who are different, Debbie is helping children learn compassion and tolerance at the very beginning of their school career.

Ruth Freedman also works to promote tolerance in her students. Ruth teaches second and third graders at the Baker Demonstration School which is part of National-Louis University in Evanston, Illinois. "My kids are so sheltered," says Ruth. I read a lot of books to them to push their thinking.

Literature is one of the most powerful vehicles we have to teach cross-cultural understanding. Through literature we can change students' thinking."

She also worked for social justice through the many occasions that presented themselves during the school year. "We let a lot of teachable moments slip past us. Instead, I'm always looking for those special opportunities." Sometimes the news media provides the springboard—for example, when a young African-American boy was recently beat up for walking in a white neighborhood in Chicago. Students discussed the prejudice that precipitates racial violence. "These kinds of conversations change our classroom life."

Ruth's students try to give back through fund raisers. They've collected clothes for a shelter for children with AIDS. They've collected toys for children who are handicapped, and books for a lending library. With the help of the student council, the whole school has worked for child abuse prevention services, the Rainforest, Oklahoma City, and The Chicago Food Conservatory. They collect money and they engage in literacy activities. "We think about why we're doing this. It leads to many discussions and further inquiry into the causes. We do a lot of reading and writing in conjunction with these projects. We're not just giving, we're learning an incredible amount.

Including special education students in regular classrooms is another way that all students will interact with a more diverse population. Kathy Feldheim teaches first grade at Sherwood School in Highland Park, Illinois. Sherwood houses the hearing impaired children in the area, as well as the physically handicapped children. Kathy had worked in conjunction with Carol Warshaw to include one hearing impaired child in her reading and writing workshop. Kathy's hearing students also learned how to sign, particularly with predictable books, poems, songs, and some of their stories.

Students from both classes also did special projects together and had fifteen minutes of recess together each day. As the hearing students learned more signs, they played with the others more often at recess. Now they play kick-ball and soccer together. They perform in plays together. They were also mainstreamed for art and gym. "The more often the students are together, the better chance for real friendships to form," says Kathy. "Now the hearing-impaired kids are even invited to birthday parties."

Kathy had more difficulty trying to convince the boys and girls to play together. "The boys told me that girls didn't know how to play sports." So Kathy took her class outside and kicked the soccer ball and hit the baseball. The boys were impressed. She led them in a discussion about what boys and girls can both do.

She brought in literature that depicted friendships between boys and girls, and girls fully participating in life. She required boys and girls to work together, and they regularly conferenced with each other. "Working together is a natural part of the day. I try not to call attention to the differences between boys and girls, but we will discuss issues that cause misperceptions.

"I don't give the kids a choice. I tell them they need to work and learn from everybody and we all have something to contribute. Sometimes I'll say to work with the person who sits next to you or across from you. I have all their names on cards, and I'll shuffle them and group them in that way. I'll have kids line up by the letters on their shirt, or by colors on their clothes. I try to monitor myself so if I call on a girl, then I next call on a boy."

Every year Kathy is particularly alert to the outsiders in her classroom. Tom was a quadriplegic who was non-physical and non-verbal. He was mainstreamed into the classroom. "My students had to learn to interact with a child who communicated with facial expressions. Even though he couldn't walk or talk, he had his own personality. My acceptance of Tom was crucial. I treated him with patience and respect and so did my students. He's been in the school for several years now and he's very accepted. He plays with the other children and is invited to the birthday parties. It's a case of familiarity. The children know him and know that there is nothing to be afraid of.

"I think that because my students come from a similar economic background, it is all the more reason to promote cross-cultural understanding. It's important that the kids don't stereotype a culture." Kathy uses literacy as her vehicle for this. She tries to read many multicultural books to her students and engage them in many literature discussions. *Tar Beach* by Faith Ringgold and *Who Belongs Here* by Margy Burns Knight are two of her favorites.

Kathy believes that there are many things that teachers can do to educate themselves. "We have to educate ourselves. We need to expose ourselves to many different cultures." Kathy suggests reading and visiting museums as points of departure. Kathy attended Elgin High School in Elgin, Illinois which was 40 percent minority at the time. "My best friends are of different cultures. That's what we need to teach our kids. There's nothing to be afraid of, but everything to gain when we embrace diversity."

"My class became very concerned about the state of the earth. I had to let the kids find their own questions for inquiry to work with me though," says fifth–grade teacher Stephanie McGlynn. Her students became interested in environmental issues by studying frogs. "They kept raising ques-

#1 deformation

Frogs are starting to deform. In other words they are gaining or losing more; legs, eys, tails, and MORE!!! Some people think it is from the environment they live in. Some don't know are here other ideas. The first big action was in Minnesota 6th grade students went out caught frogs and more than half were deformed! Scientist have studied these frogs and don't even know what it is. Will we get deformed? How long will this go on?

#2 dissapearing

Remember when you were a little kid (grown ups) and you heard the frogs day and night. Well, think now, now all the frogs are GONE!!! Were did they all go? Does to ozone layer have something to do with this? What will happen when they are all gone? All of these questions, the answer unknown.

#3 Ending

So now you know what is happening and we have to stop it! These are the canarys of our environment. Be kind to the earth and stop the dissapearing of the frogs.

Informational pamphlet created by students in Stephanie McGlynn's class.

Frog deformation concerns student

Lake Forest/ I am a fifth grade student at Central Elementary School, Lake Bluff. I am writing to inform you on the deformation and dying out of frogs. They are missing eyes, legs and many organs. They even have too many parts of their body growing in some places. It might even be happening in Lake Bluff or Lake Forest.

Some of the reasons for these things may be that the ozone layer is getting thinner each year. The ultraviolet rays could have something to do with it. Pesticides might be harming them, and also chemicals could be being dumped into their ponds and lakes. Air pollution is a possibility, and so are toxic wastes. The question is which one(s) of these possibilities are killing the frogs?

A class in Minnesota found deformed frogs and started to take some action. They told the authorities and did things like make a web page to inform people of this problem. My class is doing things like writing to newspapers, making movies and even making our own web pages.

We (my class) went on a walk in the open lands behind the water treatment center in Lake Bluff. Unfortunately we did not find any frogs. We tested the water and found that it has a high amount of ph, which is not good. We decided that this could be a reason for the frogs dying out and deforming. I think we should do something about this. After all, frogs are the canaries of our lives. Thank you.

Kate Terrill

Fifth grader Kate Terrill's letter published in the local paper.

tions." Her students informed her that they needed to learn more. "We watched a frog grow. We went to the pond and tested the water." The students were worried about the frogs' survival. They wondered what could be causing problems for frogs around the world. As a class, they generated ideas, facts, questions, and their action plan.

Stephanie's students started by sharing their ideas. Then they talked about where they could go to find the information. As they discovered the effects of pollution on the frog population, they found they wanted to educate the public. One of her students created a Web page, another wrote to the local paper and was published. Others made fliers, put up signs near the local pub, and wrote to major newspapers. Students made videos to share with other classes in the school. Two students created a lemonade stand for the friends of frogs. "It was through their own inquiry that they developed a reverence for the earth."

Mary Bencini also reflects on the power of inclusive inquiry. "When kids get done, they have questions there may not be answers for, but it raised consciousness. These questions keep coming up throughout their lives and affect the way they relate to all people throughout their lifetimes." One of her second-grade students wondered after her inquiry into the underground railroad, why the color of a person's skin has so much power. "I was amazed that a second grader asked this," says Mary.

After the underground railroad inquiry cycle was completed, Mary asked her students to write about whatever they were thinking now. "My students said they were glad that slavery was over, because it was so horrible and because Chuck was their friend and he might not have been able to be their friend." This led to the second inquiry cycle. The students read *White Socks Only* by Evelyn Coleman, a book about an African-American girl who doesn't understand the existence of separate drinking fountains. This led to more inquiry and reflection. "My students started saying that just because slavery is over, it doesn't mean that everything is okay. It doesn't mean that everybody gets a fair chance in America."

The gender issue has been increasingly scrutinized in Mary's second-grade class. "After our field day, the boys realized they could change it next time so more girls could participate." When Mary asked them what they meant, they said they should add girls' games, games that girls could do like bozo buckets and jump ropes. "The girls in my class became infuriated. They were indignant and felt that they were capable of playing any sport." This then led to a continuing discussion between the boys and girls about who was superior, boys or girls.

These girls, just as first-grade girls in the classroom I studied, wanted to be included. In both classrooms, once a problem was identified, all the students began to talk about it and to try to make things more equitable. "It has a lot to do with learning to respect each other," says Mary. "It may not be something we're studying, but it is always there. If kids learn to respect everybody in the classroom, that's the first step to respecting everybody in the world. You may not like everybody, but you can be kind. I try to show through the books we read and the inquiry we pursue that everybody can make a difference. It leads to social action in their lives."

Debbie Schreiner agrees. One of her greatest difficulties in implementing the social justice projects was the busy lives of her fifth-grade students. After school they had many demands on their time. Students had music lessons, little league, skating lessons, and ballet. This didn't include the time needed for completing homework. She's trying, though. Her class decided to visit the animal shelter and the nursing home in their community and see how they might help. This is the beginning. If we don't show children how to fit social action into their lives as adults, how will they find the time when they are adults? There are many reasons to teach for social justice, and every child is needed to create a just and equitable world.

13 | Teaching Ethics at School and at Home

All teachers interviewed for this book have a common focus: They care about all of their students. They've spent time developing a close classroom community where everyone is respected. Teaching for social justice begins with a safe and cohesive classroom community. How do teachers do this?

Walk into Janice Walter's classroom and you'll find a teacher who works tirelessly for her kids. Janice teaches at Goodwin School, in Cicero, Illinois. She is an advocate for her children, encouraging them, nudging them, and pushing them to go beyond what they thought they could. The students sit at old desks, the type where the top flips open. She arranges every four desks into working groups. Janice starts every day with the concept of "gossip." She uses it as Deborah Tannen encourages us to think about it, as a way to make connections with others. Elizabeth talks about the three-legged race she participated in during the weekend.

"It was my sister and me. We tied our legs together."

The class looks puzzled and Janice suggests that she model it with Monica. The girls stand next to each other as Elizabeth explains what to do.

"You stand like this. We didn't finish the race because Veronica's mom called her and she had to go up the stairs."

Sharing forms the center of this classroom. Students have many opportunities to tell the stories of their lives. Gossip is interwoven throughout the entire day.

Anne Swaine also teaches at Goodwin School. She teaches English as a second language for kindergarten through eighth grade. Though the school is 98 percent Hispanic, there are also Asian and Arabic children. In this primary group of children, there are three Vietnamese children, one Hispanic, and one from Lebanon. Anne's classroom was originally a closet. She shared her tiny space with her assistant. She has made maximum use of her space. Children's books crowd every available inch of shelving. Children's art work and poetry papers the walls.

On a recent day in Anne's class, Min and Nen, the two Vietnamese boys start talking almost from the moment they enter the room. All the children choose books and start talking about the pictures and telling the stories, even though they couldn't read English.

"Can I tell you something about this story?" Min asks Anne. He then tells the story by looking at the pictures. Min's story has little to do with the text or the pictures, but Anne and the other children listen attentively.

"This boy doesn't read. Can't you read? Can't you read? They kept asking him the same question. Then he went to jail," says Min.

Anne asks, "Jail?" There was nothing that looks like a jail in the picture.

Min explains, "Cause he's cross walking. He said, 'I think my memory is going.' "

Nen chimes in, "Yeah. I think it went to California."

Tu is also from Vietnam. She speaks no English and is quietly watching the exchange of the boys surrounding her. They finish the first book and are gathered around a ladybug book, talking and laughing. All of the children know the routine of the room, it's about reading and talking about books.

Anne passes out their writing journals and the students immediately get to work.

"Min, can you help me?" Anne asks.

"That's because I'm so helpful, right?" asks Min. Tu listens quietly but says nothing.

"I'm going to make Africa," declares Nen.

"I'm going to make a lion," says Min.

For the first time, Tu smiles as she draws her rooster. She starts humming as she reaches for another color.

"Do you know the song, 'Five Little Ducks?' " Anne begins to sing. The children join in. Tu starts singing the song quietly to herself. The children's high, sweet voices fill the air. As I turn my teary eyes away from them, I notice the posters on the wall. One of them says: 35th Anniversary Peace Corps, 1961-1996. The other says: "World Peace will come through the will of ordinary people like yourself." World peace begins with teachers like Anne Swaine.

Jim Coventry is particularly concerned with the outsiders in his seventh and eighth grade classrooms. "I try to create an atmosphere of tolerance," he says. "I think values like integrity are important. We talk about them. We try to live our values. We read a lot of literature and discuss it from an ethical perspective. We talk about things like, 'Who has an opinion about the story and how did the characters have strength?' This is just my opinion, but I think we need to have a dialogue about morals and ethics. We need to help kids develop a code of ethics."

Parents, Ethics, and Literacy

Traditionally, it's been the role of parents to teach children about ethics. In these times, we all need to work together to make our children's lives better. If we are bringing ethical discussions into our classrooms, we also need to support the work that parents do at home. Often, literacy can provide another dimension for this important work done by parents.

Family Films

The Weiner family lives in Philadelphia. They try to be very involved in their two sons' lives. They read books together and spend hours discussing issues. They've participated actively in school projects that emphasize social service. The religious school the boys attend emphasizes that the community projects created for the school should be carried out to emphasize each person's talents and interests. Matthew Weiner, 15, decided to write a script about the life-cycle of a Jewish family. He wrote and revised the script until he was happy with the results. Then he directed and produced the film. His mother and father, Betty and Bill, and his younger brother Adam, 10, were all featured in the film, along with the families of many of their friends. The film was rehearsed and filmed over a number of weekends. It was screened for the entire school and has been donated to the school.

The Ethical Will

Another project that the school encourages is an ethical will. The idea behind this is simple. We leave money to our children after our deaths, but what do we really leave in terms of our hopes and aspirations for the adults they will become? We might verbalize our wishes, but it is less likely that we leave a written record behind. So the writing of an ethical will emphasizes the good we see in our children and the world, and our potential as a society to achieve this good. Betty and Bill Weiner felt that it was a positive experience to sit down and write this will, and beneficial to the whole family.

Slowing Down

The Ambrose family also incorporates literacy and social justice into the fabric of their lives. Steve and Sue try to instill in their children the need to give back to the world. Their three children, ten-year-old Jordan, seven-year-old Corbett, and five-year-old Kelsey attend Catholic school. As a family, they discuss their thoughts and feelings, and problem-solving ways to deal with the conflicts in their lives. "We talk about slowing down and taking it cool. We try to look at each situation in terms of the positive and negative aspects. This is how Steve and I solve family issues so the kids see it modeled all the time," says Sue.

Sue talks about why cross-cultural education is so important for her children. "I want my kids to honor other people for who they are and what they are. Each person is unique. We're outwardly up-front about it. We live in an extraordinarily Catholic area. Our neighbor girl is Jewish and I was horrified to hear my daughter say that if she wasn't Catholic, she wasn't a good person. I understood what was happening. She was experiencing a Catholic 'groupness.' We headed it off. It began a family discussion of differences. It's a difference. It's not better or worse."

Sue describes her family as one of the most liberal in the western suburban community in which she lives. She wants to instill in her children a sense of gratefulness for their lives. "We've worked very hard to make it clear that they are lucky to live here. Most of my friends think that their kids should just have things. My kids get toys on Christmas. The rest of the year we try to give back to the community."

Volunteering

One of the ways that the Ambrose family gives back is by working at a resale shop that benefits the local battered shelter. The project began after the school asked families to donate clothes to the resale shop. Sue's family decided to volunteer at the shop. The children accompany Sue weekly in the sorting and pricing of the clothes. "When new families come to the shelter, they often need clothing. Jordan's job is to pick out toys and

The Ethical Will of Betty and William

Dear Matthew,

Though initially motivated by the assignment to write an ethical will, this task provides us with an opportunity to think about what is important to us as your parents and to crystallize what we want to communicate to you about what we feel is essential in the way we hope you live your life.

It is important for you to know that our love, support, and concern will go with you wherever life may take you. We hope that our love and guidance have provided you with a solid foundation based upon our family ideals which we have communicated through our love of family and the example of how we live our lives. We also hope that the strong secular and Jewish education with which we have provided you will be a springboard from which you can develop your own ideals and viewpoints.

We believe that within each of us is a force to do good in the world. This potential needs to be nurtured and developed and represents the part in which our Jewishness can influence our development. The ethics and ideals of our heritage that you have spent so much time learning can influence your decision-making throughout your life. The Jewish rituals and sense of community can provide a source of joy and richness but also a strength to draw upon during some of life's more challenging times.

You already have a beautiful soul, a warm, open heart, and an excellent mind. You have integrity, honesty and trustworthiness. You are very precious to us and we want you to always take care of your body, mind and soul. Your actions earn the respect of others wherever you go. We encourage you to always be true to yourself. Act in ways that you can feel proud of yourself. Act in ways that are consistent with your beliefs and don't be afraid to express your beliefs. Be realistic in your views, but always maintain a positive attitude. Remember "the cup is half-full, not half-empty." Take time to enjoy the seemingly little things in life such as the feel of a gentle wind on your face, the call of a bird, or the beauty of a blooming flower. Stress quality of work and life rather than quantity of work and material goods. Be respectful and kind to others yet do not allow them to take advantage of you. Let your choices be guided by your own sense of fairness, justice, and truth, not solely influenced by the needs or demands of others. Yet, it is also important to consider others and what help or support they may require from you.

When you look back over your life we hope that you feel that the world is a better place, even in some small way, because you were here. We certainly feel that the world is a much better place because you are here. We hope you know, too, that you are truly loved. The love we give you is our eternal gift and is our blessing. Carry this with you always.

Love,

Mom + Dad

clothes that she thinks the children will like. She's become very good at choosing them. It's one small way we make life a little easier for these children."

They also have family service projects. Besides the resale shop, they adopt families at Thanksgiving and Christmas and shop for them. They participate in clothing drive collections and government cheese distributions. They've worked with the homeless shelter and have visited a nearby retirement home. They try to tie the projects to writing whenever possible. Jordan is a prolific writer and reader. Jordan writes about children who lead many different kinds of lives. "I'm pretending and experimenting with other things that aren't my life. When you read a book, you're going into another life," she says.

Both Steve and Sue read to their children, and they buy many books for them, especially emphasizing good multicultural and feminist literature. They use the books as a springboard for discussing the world and their lives.

"We call it the pluses and the minuses. For instance, one of my daughter's friends was moving and she kept bragging about her new house. My daughter said, 'Mom, do you know how hard it is for me not to say anything?' "

"What did you do?" I ask her.

"I sympathized," says Sue, "and told her that, in our house, we don't brag about our good fortune. It's hard because so much of our culture is about money and buying. As a parent, if you don't feel emotionally mature and able to work it through, your kids will have trouble. Lots of my neighbors say that they want their kids to work through their problems, but then they don't do it."

Sue continues by talking about diversity and social justice. She feels that adults say it's important, but then do little to make it happen with their own children. If diversity is not supported at home, parents won't support the school curriculum, even when social justice is a theme in the classroom.

Blurring Gender Roles

As parents, Steve and Sue want their daughters to have the same type of opportunities as their son. At times, they have had to intervene to make sure this occurred. The uniforms at the Catholic School the children attended consisted of shirts and pants for the boys, but dresses with socks or tights for the girls. "I thought that was ridiculous," said Sue. So she organized the parents, and they asked the administration to let girls wear pants, too. It might sound like a little thing, but it was a huge issue. Now the girls can run around just like the boys.

They want their children to be comfortable with who they are. Corbett plays dress-up and has a Ken doll. Their daughter Kelsey has a natural talent for batting and catching. Sue and Steve support their children's explorations, regardless of traditional gender roles. They work to include diversity in their children's lives. They moved to a more diverse neighborhood and enrolled their children in a school that was more culturally and ethnically diverse. They continue to add to their multicultural book collection. They take their family to ethnic museums, restaurants, and events as often as possible. They also find that traveling with the children is a great way to widen perspectives.

Both the Ambrose and the Weiner families share a commitment to literacy, justice, and social service. For families like these working toward social justice, the work in schools can extend and support their vision. The Weiner's ethical will was a result of a school assignment. The Ambrose's resale shop work began with the school. The amount of work that needs to done before we have a just society is enormous. No family or teacher can do it alone. We need to work together as partners to make a difference.

The access to knowledge is now overwhelming, as it's become very easy to accumulate knowledge with computers. "Think about it," my friend Pat Eggleston says. "All you have to do is access the Internet and you can get the answer to most any question. But facts aren't enough. Victor Frankel has pointed out that prior to World War II, Germany was one of the most educated countries in the world. Some of the most educated Nazis committed the most horrific crimes. Facts alone are not enough."

What children need to learn in our classrooms is how to make facts fit human needs. We need to provide the framework that helps children pull things together and give meaning to their lives. Students need to value life and their lives. Unless you learn for human values, you're not truly educated.

We can't be afraid to teach ethics and values in our literacy programs. Morality should be included in the curriculum. Society is ever–changing and we need to be educated in accordance with change. We shouldn't ostracize unwed mothers and their children. One of my brother-in-law's friends spent his first five years in an orphanage because it was illegal in Switzerland for his unwed mother to raise her own child. When he was five, his mother rescued him from the orphanage and moved to the United States. Many lesbian and gay families are warm and loving, morally responsible, and teach ethics to their children. We need to have a larger vision for morality and ethics, one that is inconclusive and consistent with the diverse population of all the people on the planet and the many ways to live upon it.

But this new vision has to include the valuing of all life, and of every individual's right to be productive and thrive. We need to include concepts like respect, love, the right to a peaceful life, and fair and equal opportunities for all. We have done humanity a disservice when we've allowed one segment of the population to define and claim who is acceptable and who isn't, and what is ethical and what isn't.

Ethics cross all artificial boundaries and connect us to the natural world. The ecofeminist movement emphasizes the interconnectivity of all of life. We have to care and make ethical decisions about our planet, or it is likely that our planet won't survive. The human race must get beyond our divisions and start working together, to do what is right, to nourish our children, to save our earth.

Florence Krall (1994), in her book *Ecotone*, describes the ecotone as the place

"in the natural world [that] provides a dynamic interchange, becoming exceedingly complex as a cultural metaphor (p.5)." She continues:

> I have chosen the concept of ecotone, then, to represent that place of meeting and tension between diverse and sometimes conflicting aspects of our lives. Underlying the familiar cultural/Nature dichotomy is instead a webbing of gender, race, politics, economics, and spirituality that preoccupies wayfaring humans on this planet. Ecotone, that place of crossing over, provides sanctuary, solitude and peace, growth and transformation, as well as isolation and inner or outer conflict. It is all of these as well as a psycho-

logical space of natural tension where we transcend our present limitations and move to new possibilities, a time when individuation brings with it a deeper sense of interrelatedness. (p. 6)

In nature, the ecotone is the physical margin that acts as a buffer between two different ecosystems. It provides the place for transitional species to live. Seen in this light, the outsiders in our classrooms bring richness and unimagined possibilities to our classrooms. Perhaps those of us who are using literacy to teach for social justice are working in our own educational ecotone, trying out new ways of coming together, learning from our students, confronting violence and injustice and finding new ways to value all human beings. Where do we go from here? We continue bringing our work in the ecotone into the wider world, thereby transforming our lives in the process. One day, all our students will spread their wings and fly.

14 | A Final Word

How can we create social justice in a world where there seems to be so much injustice? As the teachers interviewed for this book have shown us, we do it one student at a time, one day at a time. We establish a community in our classrooms where we and our students feel safe. To give you a jump start, I've created the following list of goals and ideas for you to use as you see fit. Don't forget to add your own!

1. Strive to make your classroom as comfortable and safe as possible. Talk to the students about the value of each person and the importance of hearing everyone's opinions in the classroom. Help students embrace diversity in their lives.

   a) Treat all people with respect. Teach your students to do the same.

   b) Watch the words you use to describe others accurately but positively.

   c) Teach peace and conflict resolution in your classroom. Share the work of those who have preceded you. Peace has always seemed elusive, but it is within reach. We need to give our kids the skills to negotiate conflict and find peaceful ways to resolve arguments.

2. Become an agent of change in your classroom and your school. Encourage your school to communicate with other communities. Do the groundwork that would encourage more interaction.

3. Risk arguments. If you find yourself in situations where people make racist, prejudiced, anti-Semitic, or homophobic remarks, speak out. Confront prejudice.

4. Educate your community about many cultures, poverty, and oppression. Bring in speakers to speak at faculty meetings and inservice days. Read books together. Visit museums. View films. Make it your personal mission to learn more about cultures and people who face oppression.

5. Form coalitions with city schools. If you work in suburban or rural situations, make connections with teachers in urban areas. Find out how to help. Exchange e-mail addresses or set up list-serves or chat rooms.

6. Form coalitions with suburban and rural schools. We have a lot to offer schools in other situations. Reach out to them.

7. Do research in your classroom. Teacher research is a powerful way to explore how diversity affects classroom life. Then tell your story by publication.

8. Visit museums. There are museums that feature cultures and others that have exhibits on specific cultural groups. There are museums that focus on African-Americans, Mexicans, Jews, Poles, Ukrainians, the Irish, and Lithuanians, to name a few. Their exhibits offer continuing opportunities for education.

9. Concentrate on one culture for a while; there are many things to do. Turn on the television. If you concentrate on the Hispanic culture, for example, there are television and radio stations in Spanish. Even if you don't understand the language, there are many things you can pick up about the culture. Read books (in translation if necessary) by Hispanic authors. Visit Hispanic museums, restaurants, and areas of the city. Make friends with people from the many Hispanic cultures.

10. Use cross-cultural literature in your classroom every day. This is a powerful statement that you can make for your kids. You are saying that you value different cultures so much that you can't let a day go by without learning something new or sharing a story about another culture.

11. Incorporate literature discussions about multicultural books in classrooms.

12. Become pen pals with a class from another cultural group. Arrange for joint projects that allow each class to have the opportunity to teach the other. Have joint experiences so the students can meet each other. Becoming friends is one of the best ways to counter prejudice. Make sure students from the lower socio-economic group can be in positions of teaching and sharing information with the more affluent students. You don't want this to be a situation where the affluent kids think they are doing a good deed, have nothing to learn, and feel sorry for the children. You need to create situations where all students are valued and have equal status.

13. Use the Inclusive Inquiry Cycle in your classroom.

14. Encourage students to ask questions like "Why is this?", "Who does it benefit?", and "Who is left out?"

15. Show the film, *It's Elementary: Talking About Gay Issues in School* to your faculty.

16. Confront name-calling of all types in school.

17. Confront gay-bashing. Prejudice against gay and lesbian people is already going on. If we do nothing, we are sending the message that it is acceptable to oppress them in school. There are gay children in schools who witness this behavior and are terrified. Children in lesbian and gay families are also receiving negative and scary messages about their families. Gay-bashing has to be stopped, and this can be done only through education.

18. Invite lesbian and gay speakers to your school. Let children ask questions to breakdown stereotypes.

19. Share literature that includes lesbian and gay individuals and families.

20. Do a language project on the origin of all kinds of pejoratives like *gimp*, *queer*, and *gay*.

21. Study the contributions that lesbian and gay people have made both in modern times and throughout history. There are books available that describe many of these contributions.

22. Talk about this issue as it comes up in the classroom. *This is not a sexual discussion, but it is about prejudice and discrimination*. It's vital that the discussions start when students are young, in elementary school, to break down the misconceptions and abuse.

23. Encourage "hate-free zones" rather than restricting students' language. Hate-free zones are safe places where prejudice and intolerance are not allowed. It's not enough to stop the name-calling without the understanding that comes from teaching for tolerance.

24. Include gay and lesbian issues every time you discuss multicultural themes.

25. Have schools safe enough so that teachers can come out. Both students and teachers would benefit. All students would realize that they know someone who is gay or lesbian. Gay and lesbian children would have some positive role models that could give them hope about their own lives. The United States Department of Health and Human Service estimates that as many as 30 percent of all teen suicides are committed by lesbian and gay teenagers (Uribe 1996). It is time we combat homophobia now.

26. Fight poverty in every way you can. Poverty cripples so many lives. We all need to do what we can to end it. Find out about food distributions and pantries. Volunteer at homeless shelters. Get involved at political levels.

27. Join literacy projects. Help kids and adults read and write better.

28. Support Head Start programs, drop-in centers, and family programs that promote literacy. Find out how to help and do something.

29. Support private schools that are dedicated to promoting peace and interracial harmony. These schools exist in many communities.

30. Lobby for smaller class sizes. Unfortunately, there is a gap between urban and suburban schools in the areas of funding, educational opportunities, and class size. Both the Texas and California state legislatures have passed laws mandating class size at reasonable levels. This means that the minute the class size goes over the minimum number, a new teacher is brought in. Portable classrooms are provided to accommodate the new classes. It makes sense that students will get more attention in smaller classes. State legislatures are mandating all kinds of measures that affect teaching, particularly testing. It's time that teachers become political, speaking out against negative measures and promoting more positive bills.

31. Continue your political work by explaining to the public how you are teaching and why. Contact newspapers, radio, television, and businesses, through projects with various civic groups and organizations. Many local newspapers and public access cable television stations are constantly looking for "good-news" stories.

32. Promote tolerance in yourself, your students, and your communities.

33. Learn to live and truly celebrate diversity and multiple perspectives in your own life.

34. Do the best you can, and try not to burn out in your present situation. Work to keep your integrity, and celebrate the small successes that are present every day in your life.

35. Make room for all families on administrative forms. Change exclusive language, add extra lines, work so that all the members in the stepfamilies, extended families, and alternative families are included.

36. Draw some extra lines on the family trees. Be sensitive to the kinds of assignments offered, with two or three variations or choices. You don't know if there is a father absent or two fathers present.

These are only a few suggestions to get started, but if we all begin to work through the list, who knows how many lives we can touch?

A

When I Got Shot
By Erick Padilla

I was cutting my hair with my brothers friend. When Raul called me and asked me if I wanted to go to his house. I told him I would go after I took a shower. I asked my parents if I could go, and they said, "yeah to come back in 2 hrs."

When I got to Raul's house he asked me if I wanted to see something cool I said "yes", He took me to his room and took out a 38 hand gun. I asked him, "Why do you have it"? he didn't answer. So he took out the bullets from the carriage and put 2 of the bullets back into the gun. He told me, let's go outside. I said, "al right."

We went thru the back door, I saw a rabbit and I threw a small rock at it and missed. I stood by his basement window, I heard two clicks from the gun coming from behind me. I turned around, I saw a gun, heard a click and then boom! Seconds past, I felt a burning inside of me, I was dizzy. I didn't know what happened. Suddenly Raul pulled my jacket and brought me into his house. And I remember that he told me, "I'm sorry, I'm sorry," teil then it was a drive by. Raul shouted to his father, "Erick got shot!" He quickly came over and walked me over to the coach, and laid me down.

I feltt this burning by my chest. I saw this black around my sweater. Rauls father took off my sweater and there was a hole by my chest! I said fuck! I've been shot. Lights were flickering by the window from the ambulence. Paramedics came in and laid me on a red stretcher, and that's when I heard my brothers voice, "I'm Ericks brother, let me in!" He began swearing because they wouldn't let him in. After that they took me out and put me in the ambulance and said that my mom is coming. But she never did.

As we were in the ambulance
the paramedic said, "Don4 fall
asleep, because you might not
wake up." I said "I know man!"
I knew that because I watched
"Cops." They told me not to worry,
that I would live, and that we
would be there in 7 minutes. I laid
there, staring and moving my fingers
waiting to get to the hospital.

I was feeling something burning inside of
me and I felt like I couldn't breath
for a split second, but when they were taking
me to the hospital I was feeling itchy.
when we got into the hospital they put something
so I will go to sleep. When I woke up I
was in a room with my parents. I was
feeling really weird and I couldn't talk
that loud because I had staples. But I
tried to tell my dad that Raul shot me
he heard me and asked me "Why?"
I said I don't know, but then I was
feeling bad.   - When I talked, my
chest was hurting.

It was pretty boring in the hospital because
everyday they always woke me up at 4:00 Am.
I always saw movies or tv. And when I wanted
I could just call the nurse to give me
juices or food. My parents or my brother
usually came to visit me or to bring me
movies. They always tried to make me smile
but I never did because I couldn't even
talk that loud.

I was really mad and thinking that I'm
going to have to stay really long in the
hospital. But when my doctor came in I asked
her how long will I have to stay in, she said
in about a week or less—
I was in for 6 days.

When I was going to get out of
the hospital I was really happy
but they told me that I had to
eat some nasty food. I told them
"Why"? they said, "eat it or your
staying for Christmas." So I told
them, "OK". I ate the fries and I
threw away the really nasty looking
food. I almost threw up but I
didn4. Later, around 4:30 pm, they
said, "I had to wait for my
doctor". I said "OK" and waited like
2 hours. She finally came and told me
I could leave, I said, "thank you."
I walked quickly to the car and
we went home on Christmas Eve.

The day it was christmas it
was boring because I couldn4
come out or play with my dogs. The
only thing I did was open my
boring presents. To see if there

were good things but there was
nothing good no new shoes. Just
a stretch man that broke, so then I
went to sleep, because it was boring.
Later, when I woke up I was
watching a movie and then when it
was getting stupid I put on the
sega and started playing for like
2 hours. If I didn't get shot I wouldn't
have these staples in me. And I would
be playing outside. It was a pretty
boring Christmas and New Years.
So then I told my self should I
stay up or not then I said I'm
going to bed.

I was
going back to school, because I
was going to see my friends again. But
some of my friends were differently.
They were treating me like I had,
power or something. They would be like,
"What happened", "who shot you?" They were
making jokes to make me laugh. 7th +
8th graders that didn't know me, came
up and talked to me. I was surprised
because I never used to talk to them.
They thought I was cool just because I
got shot. But It wasn't cool, if I go back
in time, I wouldn't of gone to Raul's
house. I still hadn't seen Raul or talked
with him.
    I wondered why Raul shot me. We
knew each other for 5 or 6 years. I
didn't want to talk to him, I wouldn't know
what to say to him.

The day I got my staples off my
doctor got out some sharp scissors
and picked them off. It only hurt
a little bit because she did it really
fast, I looked at it. It looked nasty,
like it was going to open!
But it never did, However, when she
got to the last five staples it hurt
because they were deep inside my
skin. Afterwords my doctor told
me not to lift anything just let
my mom do it. Everyday I had to
change my bandgages, It hurt
because it was peeling my skin
off.

I couldn't play around because the
wound might open. I was off from
school for 3 weeks, so I just sat home
and was bored. I watched the same
shows and couldn't wait to get back to school.

One day while I was playing Sega, a
police officer called and asked if he could
come over to hear my side of the story.
When he came he was asking questions on
how it happened. I told him the whole story,
    The police officer told me that he knew
it wasn't a drive-by because there was bullet
powder in my jacket. (If it was a drive-by
there wouldn't be any powder.)
    He asked me if I knew who had shot
me, I told him "yeah, Raul did It." He
said "hold on" and called the other police officers.
Then he left to go to Raul's house to ask
him questions. As a was leaving he said I
would be receiving a court date. I thought
as he left, that Raul would n't tell the
truth, and would lie about shooting me.
    A couple of days later, the police
officer called my parents and said
Raul had confessed to shooting me,
I was surprised because I thought that

143

he would keep on lying. Now we wont have to go to court and start screaming at each other. Two weeks later we got the paper that said that we have to go to court in a month. I was real nervous.

I knew when I would go to court that I would finally see Raul. Some people had told me that Raul really wanted to shoot me. But one of his gang friends said that he didnt know it was loaded and that he was just checking it. He was given the gun by one of his gang friends. I dont know why they had given him a gun, he thinks differently than others. He is weird. Why would someone trust him with a gun? I didnt know any of these answers and I wanted to know soon.

I was nerves because I have never been in court in my whole life so when they calledusin I went in with my parents and my brother. Well, the judge asked Raul if he brought the gun to school. He said "yes" and they were asking different questions. When court finished my parents still have to go to court, because the unpaid hospital bills. So after we got out of court Raul's parents were talking to my dad that Raul did not know that the gun was loded. So then after a long time I told my dad to give me the keys then we leaft.

My Hero

My hero is my brother because everyday he tells me to stay out of gangs. I always listen to him. Another hero is my doctor, because if it wasn't for her, I would have died.

The End

By Erick

B

References

Including other books and articles not listed in Appendixes

Barnes, Douglas. 1976. *From Communication to Curriculum*. New York: Viking Penquin.

Bogdan, R. and Biklen, S. 1982. *Qualitative Research for Education*. Boston: Allyn & Bacon.

Bruner, Jerome S. 1978. "The role of dialogue in language acquisition." In *The Child's Concept of Language*, A. Sinclair, R. Jarvelle, and W. Levelt (Eds.), (241–256). New York: Springer-Verlag.

Crafton, Linda. 1991. *Whole Language: Getting Started . . . Moving Forward*. Katonah, New York: Richard C. Owen Publishers, Inc.

Dudley-Marling, Curt and Sharon Murphy. "A Political Critique of Remedial Reading Programs: The Example of Reading Recovery." *The Reading Teacher* (50)6 460–469.

Edelsky, C. 1994. "Education for Democracy." *Language Arts*. (71) 252–257.

Ellsworth, Elizabeth. 1989. "Why Doesn't This Feel Empowering? Working through the Repressive Myths of Critical Pedagogy." *Harvard Educational Review*. (59) 297–324.

Falk, Jane. 1979. *"The Duet as a Conversational Process."* Unpublished doctoral dissertation, Princeton University, Princeton, NJ.

Hulsebosch, Patricia and Mari Koerner. 1996. "Preparing Teachers to Work with Children of Gay and Lesbian Parents. *Journal of Teacher Education* 47(5) 347–354.

Leland, Christine H. and Jerome C. Harste. 1994. "Multiple Ways of Knowing: Curriculum in a New Key." *Language Arts* (71) 337–345.

Lensmire, Timothy. 1992. *When Children Write*. New York: Teachers College Press.

McNally, Terrance. 1995. *Master Class*. Production at Shubert Theatre, Chicago, IL, February, 1997.

Moll, Luis C. and Norma Gonzalez. 1994. "Lessons from Research with Language-Minority Children." *Journal of Reading Behavior* (26)4 439–456.

Myers, J. 1992. "The Social Contexts of School and Personal Literacy. *Reading Research Quarterly* (27) 297–333.

Rowe, Mary B. 1987. "Wait-time: Slowing Down May Be a Way of Speeding Up." *American Educator* (2)1 38–43.

Singer, B. L. and D. Deschamps, D. (Eds.) 1994. *Gay and Lesbian Stats*. New York: New Press.

Smith, Frank. 1988. *Joining the Literacy Club*. Portsmouth, NH.: Heinemann. Spradley, J. 1979. *The Ethnographic Interview*. New York: Holt, Rinehart, & Winston.

Swift, J.N., Swift, P.R. and C.T. Gooding. 1988. "Questions and Wait Time." In *Questioning and Discussion: A Multidisciplinary Study*, J.T. Dillon (Ed.). Norwood, NJ: Ablex Publishing Corporation, 192–211.

Uribe, Virginia. 1996. "Project 10: A School-based Outreach to Gay and Lesbian Youth." In *Open Lives Safe Schools*, Donovan R. Walling (Ed.). Bloomington, IN: Phi Delta Kappa Educational Foundation.

Vygotsky, Lev. 1962. *Thought and Language*. Cambridge, MA: The M.I.T. Press.

Wells, G. and G.L. Chang-Wells. 1992. *Constructing Knowledge Together*. Portsmouth, NH: Heinemann.

C

Who Is Invited to Share in My Classroom?

Write yes or no after each question. When appropriate, expand on your response to the questions.

In my classroom:

1. Does everyone get along?
2. Is anyone left out?
3. Do boys and girls voluntarily choose to work together often?
4. Do boys and girls voluntarily choose to play together often?
5. Are there outsiders?
6. Is everyone's family respected?
7. Do I call on girls as often as boys?
8. Do I praise girls as often as boys?
9. Do I give girls as much attention as boys?
10. Are girls invited to share just as often as are boys?
11. Are girls' interests, conversational styles, writing and literary styles honored as often as are boys' interests, conversational styles, and writing and literary styles?

Statements that I know to be true about my classroom. Please answer yes or no to each statement.

1. I affirm girls' responses in academic areas, especially math and science, as much as I affirm boys' responses.
2. I have no boys' or girls' lines in my classroom.
3. We do not line up for recess or the bathroom separated by gender.
4. My children are never made to line up.
5. I always call children into lines by attributes other than gender, such as the color of the clothing they are wearing.
6. I never give assignments that would embarrass my students.
7. I never give assignments that would make students feel like outsiders in my classroom.
8. I am aware of all my children's family situations, and affirm them in my classroom.
9. There are no outsiders in my classroom.
10. I know what to do with outsiders in my classroom.
11. I affirm the ethnic, racial, and/or cultural diversity of all my students and their families.
12. Multicultural education means more in my classroom than just studying a culture for a day or a month, or having a food festival, or adding one new content area.
13. Children experience equity and democracy in my classroom.
14. Students understand and live the concept of social justice in my classroom.
15. Students work for social justice in my classroom.

D | How Well Do You Know Your Students' Home Lives?

1. I know every student's family structure.
2. I can name the students in my classroom who are living in stepfamilies.
3. I can name the students in my classroom who are living in alternative families (parents who are same–sex couples; communal families).
4. I can name the students living in bi–racial families.
5. I can name the students living in poverty conditions.
6. I can name the students who have been affected by gangs.
7. I can name the students whose homes have been burned in a fire.
8. I can name the students who have been affected by domestic violence.
9. I can cite the different races and cultures in my classroom.
10. I can name the languages spoken at home by my students.
11. I can name some of the pressing social issues that affect my students.
12. I can refer my students to some of the children's books that deal with any of the above topics.
13. I can name some of the ways I can invite parents in to enrich my literacy curriculum and to help students make connections between their home and school cultures.

E

Children's Books by Possible Themes

African American

Author	Title	Publisher City	Publisher Name	Date
Adoff, Arnold	Black Is Brown Is Tan	New York	Harpercrest	1973
Arnot, Kathleen	African Myths and Legends	New York	Oxford University Press	1990
Atkinson, Mary	Maria Teresa	New York	Lollipop Power	1979
Barber, Barbara E.	Saturday at the New You	New York	Lee & Low	1994
Barrett, Mary Brigin	Sing to the Stars	Boston	Little Brown	1994
Bontemps, A. and L. Hughes	Popo and Fifina	New York	Oxford University Press	1993
Bryan, Ashley	The Dancing Granny	New York	Aladdin Paperbacks	1977
Buffet, Jimmy and S. Jane	The Jolly Mon	San Diego	Harcourt Brace	1988
Cameron, Amy	The Stories Julian Tells	New York	Alfred A . Knopf	1981
Church, Vivian	Colors Around Me	New York	Afro-American Distr. Co.	1974
Clifton, Lucille	Don't You Remember?	New York	E.P. Dutton	1973
Clifton, Lucille	Everett Anderson's Friend	New York	Henry Holt	1992
Clifton, Lucille	Everett Anderson's Goodbye	New York	Henry Holt	1983
Coleman, Evelyn	White Socks Only	Morton Grove, IL	Whitman	1996
Curtis, Christopher Paul	The Watsons Go to Birmingham—1963	New York	Delacorte Press	1995
Davis, Burke	Black Heroes of the American Revolution	New York	Harcourt Brace	1992
Duplechan, Larry	Blackbird	New York	St. Martin's	1986
Farmer, Nancy	A Girl Named Disaster	New York	Orchard Books	1996
Fenner, Carol	Yolanda's Genius	New York	Aladdin Paperbacks	1995
Fox, Paula	The Slave Dancer	New York	Dell Publishing	1973
Greenfield, Eloise	Daydreamers	New York	Dial Books	1981
Greenfield, Eloise	Night on Neighborhood Street	New York	Dial Books	1991
Greenfield, Eloise	Nathaniel Talking	New York	Black Butterfly	1988
Greenfield, Eloise	Honey, I Love	New York	Harper & Row	1978
Hamilton, Virginia	The Magical Adventures of Pretty Pearl	New York	Harper & Row	1983
Hathorn, Libby	Way Home	New York	Crown Publishers	1994
Hopkinson, Deborah	Sweet Clara and the Freedom Quilt	New York	Alfred A. Knopf	1993
Hru, Dakari	Joshua's Masai Mask	New York	Lee & Low	1993
Hughes, Langston	Black Misery	New York	Oxford University Press	1994
Hughes, Langston and M. Meltzer	A Pictorial History of the Negro in America	New York	Crown Publishers	1963
Johnson-Feelings, Dianne ed.	The Best of The Brownies' Book	New York	Oxford University Press	1996
Krull, Kathleen	Wilma Unlimited	New York	Harcourt Brace	1996
Levine, Ellen	Freedom's Children	New York	Putnam	1993
Lorbiecki, Marybeth	Just One Flick of a Finger	New York	Dial Books	1996
Lyons, Mary E.	Letters From a Slave Girl: The Story of Harriet Jacobs	New York	Aladdin	1996

Author	Title	Publisher City	Publisher Name	Date
McKissack, Patricia C.	*Mirandy and Brother Wind*	New York	The Trumpet Club	1988
Meltzer, Milton	*Underground Man*	New York	Harcourt Brace	1990
Mendez, Phil	*The Black Snowman*	New York	Scholastic	1989
Miller, William	*Zora Hurston and the Chinaberry Tree*	New York	Lee & Low	1994
Mollel, Tololwa	*The Orphan Boy*	New York	Clarion Books	1990
Meltzer, Milton	*Underground Man*	Orlando, FL	Harcourt Brace	1972
Nikola-Lisa W.	*Bein' with You This Way*	New York	Lee & Low	1994
Parks, Rosa	*I Am Rosa Parks*	New York	Dial Books	1997
Parks, Rosa & Reed Gregory J.	*Dear Mrs. Parks: A Dialogue With Today's Youth*	New York	Lee & Low Books	1996
Paulsen, Gary	*Nightjohn*	New York	Bantam Doubleday Dell	1993
Polacco, Patricia	*Pink and Say*	New York	Philomel Books	1994
Ringgold, Faith	*Aunt Harriet's Underground Railroad in the Sky*	New York	Crown Publishers	1992
Ringgold, Faith	*My Dreams of Martin Luther King*	New York	Crown Publishers	1995
Ringgold, Faith	*Tar Beach*	New York	Crown Publishers	1991
Ringgold, Faith	*Dinner at Aunt Connie's House*	New York	Hyperion Books for Children	1993
Silverman, Jerry	*Just Listen to This Song I'm Singing*	New York	Millbrook Press	1996
Smalls-Hector, Irene	*Irene and the Big, Fine Nickel*	Boston	Little Brown	1991
Staples, Suzanne Fisher	*Dangerous Skies*	New York	Farrar Straus and Giroux	1996
Tate, Eleanora E.	*The Secret of Gumbo Grove*	New York	Bantam Books	1988
Taylor, Mildred D.	*Let the Circle Be Unbroken*	New York	Puffin Books	1981
Taylor, Mildred D.	*The Road to Memphis*	New York	Puffin Books	1992
Turner, Glennette Tilley	*Running for our Lives*	New York	Holiday House	1994
Turner, Robyn Montana	*Faith Ringgold*	New York	Little Brown	1993
Williams, Shirley Anne	*Working Cotton*	San Diego	Harcourt Brace	1992
Woodson, Jacqueline	*From the Notebooks of Melanin Sun*	New York	The Blue Sky Press	1995
Yashima, Taro	*Umbrella*	New York	Puffin Books	1985

Aging

Author	Title	Publisher City	Publisher Name	Date
Farber, Norma	*How Does it Feel to be Old?*	New York	E.P. Dutton	1990
Fleischman, Paul	*The Borning Room*	New York	HarperCollins	1991
Fox, Mem	*Wilfrid Gordon McDonald Partridge*	Australia	Kane/Miller	1984
Johnson, Angela	*When I Am Old With You*	New York	Orchard Books	1990
Polacco, Patricia	*Mrs. Katz and Tush*	New York	Bantam Books	1992
Varley, Susan	*Badger's Parting Gifts*	New York	Lothrop, Lee & Shepard	1984
Walker, Alice	*To Hell with Dying*	San Diego	Harcourt Brace	1993
Wild, Margaret	*Remember Me*	Niles, IL	Albert Whitman & Co.	1990
Wilhelm, Hans	*I'll Always Love You*	New York	Crown Publishers	1985

Asian

Author	Title	Publisher City	Publisher Name	Date
Baillie, Allan	*Little Brother*	New York	Puffin Books	1985
Dejong, Meindert	*The House of Sixty Fathers*	New York	Harper & Row	1956
Demi	*Liang and the Magic Paintbrush*	New York	Henry Holt	1980

Author	Title	Publisher City	Publisher Name	Date
Friedman, Ina R.	*How My Parents Learned to Eat*	Boston	Houghton Mifflin	1984
Kahukiwa, Robyn	*Taniwha*	New York	Penguin Group	1986
Lewis, Elizabeth Foreman	*Young Fu of the Upper Yangtze*	New York	Dell Publishing	1932
Mochizuki, Ken	*Heros*	New York	Lee & Low	1995
San Souci, Robert D.	*The Samurai's Daughter*	New York	Dial Books	1992
Say, Allan	*Grandfather's Journey*	New York	Houghton Mifflin	1993
Yep, Laurence	*The Star Fisher*	New York	Puffin Books	1991
Yep, Laurence	*The Serpent's Children*	New York	Harper & Row	1984

Families

Author	Title	Publisher City	Publisher Name	Date
Adoff, Arnold	*Black Is Brown Is Tan*	New York	Harpercrest	1973
Atkinson, Mary	*Maria Teresa*	New York	Lollipop Power	1979
Bunting, Eve	*A Day's Work*	New York	Clarion Books	1994
Bunting, Eve	*Going Home*	New York	Joanna Cotler Books	1996
Bunting. Eve	*The Wednesday Surprise*	New York	Clarion Books	1989
Chall, Marsha Wilson	*Up North at the Cabin*	New York	Lothrop, Lee & Shepard	1992
Erlbach, Arlene	*The Families Book*	Minneapolis	Free Spirit	1996
Friedman, Ina R.	*How My Parents Learned to Eat*	Boston	Houghton Mifflin	1984
Galloway, Priscilla	*Jennifer Has Two Daddies*	Toronto	The Women's Press	1985
Geras, Adele	*My Grandmother's Stories*	New York	Borzoi Book	1990
Grossman, P. and E.O. Sanchez	*Saturday Market*	New York	Lothrop, Lee & Shepard	1994
Hazen, Nancy	*Grown-ups Cry Too*	New York	Lollipop Power	1973
Jenness, Aylette	*Families*	Boston	Houghton Mifflin	1990
Jonas, An	*When You Were a Baby*	New York	Greenwillow	1991
Joose, Barbara	*Mama, Do You Love Me?*	New York	StoryTime	1993
MacLachlan, Patricia	*Journey*	New York	Dell Publishing	1991
Melmed, Laura Krauss	*I Love You So Much*	New York	Lothrop, Lee & Shepard	1993
Newman, Leslea	*Heather Has Two Mommies*	Boston	Allyson Wonderland	1989
Nye, Naomi Shihab	*Sitti's Secret*	New York	Four Winds Press	1994
Ormerod, Jan	*Sunshine*	New York	Mulberry Books	1990
Reyher, Becky	*My Mother is the Most Beautiful Woman in the World*	New York	William Morrow	1945
Say, Allan	*Grandfather's Journey*	New York	Houghton Mifflin	1993
Simon, Norma	*All Kinds of Families*	Niles, IL	Albert Whitman	1987
Simon, Norma	*Why Am I Different?*	Niles, IL	Albert Whitman	1993
Willhoite, Michael	*Daddy's Roommate*	Boston	Allyson Wonderland	1990
Williams, Vera B.	*More, More, More, Said the Baby*	New York	Greenwillow Books	1990
Zolotow, Charlotte Shapiro	*William's Doll*	New York	Harpercrest	1987

Folk Tales

Author	Title	Publisher City	Publisher Name	Date
Bryan, Ashley	*The Dancing Granny*	New York	Aladdin Paperbacks	1977
Buffett, Jimmy & S. Jane	*The Jolly Mon*	San Diego	Harcourt Brace	1988
Chapman, Carol	*The Tale of Meshka the Kvetch*	New York	Dutton Children's	1980
Cohen, Caron Lee	*The Mud Pony*	New York	Scholastic	1988
Croll, Carolyn	*Too Many Babas*	New York	Harper Collins	1994
de Paola, Tomie	*Fin M'Coul*	New York	Holiday House	1981

Author	Title	Publisher City	Publisher Name	Date
dePaola, Tomie	Strega Nona	New York	Scholastic	1975
Dejong, Meindert	The House of Sixty Fathers	New York	Harper & Row	1956
Demi	Liang and the Magic Paintbrush	New York	Henry Holt	1980
Esbensen, Barbara Juster	The Great Buffalo Race	Boston	Little Brown	1994
Gilman, Phoebe	Something from Nothing	New York	Scholastic	1992
Jeffers, Susan	Brother Eagle, Sister Sky	New York	Dial Books	1991
McKissack, Patricia C.	Mirandy and Brother Wind	New York	The Trumpet Club	1988
Mollel, Tololwa	The Orphan Boy	New York	Clarion Books	1990
Polacco, Patricia	Babushka Baba Yaga	New York	Philomel Books	1993

Gay & Lesbian

Author	Title	Publisher City	Publisher Name	Date
Bauer, Marion Dane	Am I Blue?	New York	HarperCollins	1994
Bosche, Susanne	Jenny Lives with Eric and Martin	London	Gay Men's Press	1983
Elwin, R. & M. Paulse	Asha'a Mums	Toronto	The Woman's Press	1990
Erlbach, Arlene	The Families Book	Minneapolis	Free Spirit	1996
Jordan, Mary Kate	Losing Uncle Tim	Niles, IL	Albert Whitman & Co.	1989
Kerr, M.E.	Deliver us from Evie	New York	HarperCollins	1994
Koertge, Ron	The Arizona Kid	New York	Avon Books	1989
Newman, Leslea	Gloria Goes to Gay Pride	Boston	Allyson Wonderland	1991
Newman, Leslea	Heather Has Two Mommies	Boston	Allyson Wonderland	1989
Valentine, Johnny	The Duke Who Outlawed Jelly Beans	Boston	Allyson Wonderland	1991
Willhoite, Michael	Families: A Coloring Book	Boston	Allyson Wonderland	1991
Wilhoite, Michael	Daddy's Roommate	Boston	Allyson Wonderland	1990
Woodson, Jacqueline	Melanin Sun	New York	The Blue Sky Press	1995

Hispanic

Author	Title	Publisher City	Publisher Name	Date
Ada, Alma Flor	The Gold Coin	New York	Aladdin Books	1991
Ada, Alma Flor	My Name is Maria Isabel	New York	Simon & Schuster	1995
Altman, Linda Jacobs	Amelia's Road	New York	Lee & Low	1993
Anzaldua, Gloria	Friends From the Other Side	San Francisco	Children's Book Press	1995
Becerra de Jenkins, Lyll	The Honorable Prison	New York	Puffin Books	1989
Bunting, Eve	A Day's Work	New York	Clarion Books	1994
Bunting, Eve	Going Home	New York	Joanna Cotler Books	1996
Buss, Fran Leeper	Journey of the Sparrows	New York	Dell Publishing	1991
Carlson, Lori M.	Cool Salsa	New York	Fawcett Juniper Books	1994
Castaneda, Omar S.	Abuela's Weave	New York	Lee & Low	1993
Catalano, J.	The Mexican Americans	New York	Chelsea House Publishers	1996
Cisneros, Sandra	Hairs	New York	Alfred A. Knopf	1984
Dorros, Arthur	Isla	New York	Dutton Children's Books	1995
Dorros, Arthur	Abuela	New York	Houghton Mifflin	1994
Fern, Eugene	Pepito's Story	New York	Yarrow Press	1993
Grossman, P. and E. O. Sanchez	Saturday Market	New York	Lothrop, Lee & Shepard	1994
Haggerty, Mary Elizabeth	A Crack in the Wall	New York	Lee & Low	1993
Howard, Elizabeth Fitzgerald	Papa Tells Chita a Story	New York	Simon & Schuster	1995
Hughes, L. and A. Bontemps	The Pasteboard Bandit	New York	Oxford University Press	1997
Paulsen, Gary	The Crossing	New York	Dell Publishing	1987
Simon, Norma	What Do I Do? Que Hago	Niles, IL	Albert Whitman	1969

Author	Title	Publisher City	Publisher Name	Date
Soto, Gary	*Too Many Tamales*	New York	G.P. Putnam's Sons	1996
Torres, Leyla	*Saturday Sancocho*	New York	Farrar, Straus, & Giroux	1995
Westridge Young Writer's	*Kids Explore America's Hispanic Heritage*	Santa Fe, NM	John Muir Publishers	1992

Holocaust

Author	Title	Publisher City	Publisher Name	Date
Bachrach, Susan	*Tell Them We Remember*	Boston	Little Brown	1994
Bishop, Claire Huchet	*Twenty and Ten*	New York	Puffin Books	1952
Briggs, Raymond	*When the Wind Blows*	New York	Schocken Books	1982
Children from Terezen	*I Never Saw Another Butterfly*	New York	Schocken Books	1978
Frank, Anne	*Anne Frank: The Diary of a Young Girl*	New York	Pocket Books	1952
Frank, Anne	*Anne Frank's Tales from the Secret Annex*	New York	Pocket Books	1949
Greenfeld, Howard,	*The Hidden Children*	New York	Ticknor & Field	1993
Hoestlandt, Jo	*Star of Fear, Star of Hope*	New York	Walker and Company	1993
Innocenti, Roberto	*Rose Blanche*	Mankato, MN	Creative Education, Inc.	1985
Kohner, Hannah and Walter	*Hannah and Walter: A Love Story*	New York	Warner Books	1985
Kuper, Jack	*Child of the Holocaust*	New York	Signet Books	1967
Lowry, Lois	*Number the Stars*	Boston, MA	Houghton Mifflin	1989
Matas, Carol	*Daniel's Story*	New York	Scholastic	1993
Orgel, Doris	*The Devil in Vienna*	New York	Puffin Books	1978
Reiss, Johanna	*The Upstairs Room*	New York	Bantam Books	1972
Tec, Nechama	*Dry Tears*	New York	Oxford University Press	1982
van der Rol, R. and V. R.	*Anne Frank: Beyond the Diary*	New York	Puffin Books	1993
Wild, M. & Vivas, J.	*Let the Celebrations Begin!*	Norwood, South Australia	Omnibus Books	1991
Yolen, Jane	*The Devil's Arithmetic*	New York	Penguin Group	1988

Homelessness

Author	Title	Publisher City	Publisher Name	Date
Ackerman, Karen	*The Leaves in October*	New York	Salamander	1995
Bunting, Eve	*Fly Away Home*	New York	Clarion Books	1991
Chekhov, Anton	*Kashtanka*	New York	Gulliver Books	1995
DiSalvo-Ryan, DyAnne	*Uncle Willie and the Soup Kitchen*	New York	Morrow Junior Books	1991
Evans, Douglas	*So What Do You Do*	New York	Front Street Press	1997
Fox, Paula	*Monkey Island*	New York	Orchard Books	1991
Greenberg, Elliott Keith	*Erik is Homeless*	Minneapolis	Lerner Publications	1992
Guthrie, Donna	*A Rose for Abby*	Nashville	Abington Press	1988
Holman, Felice	*The Wild Children*	New York	Puffin Books	1985
Kroloff, Rabbi Charles A.	*54 Ways You Can Help the Homeless*	New York	Hugh Lauter Levin Assoc.	1993
Paterson, Katherine	*Lyddie*	New York	Puffin Books	1991
Polacco, Patricia	*I Can Hear the Sun*	New York	Philomel Books	1996
Rylant, Cynthia	*An Angel for Solomon Singer*	New York	Orchard Books	1992
Skelton, Mora	*The Baritone Cat*	New York	Stoddart Kids	1996
Spohn, Kate	*Broken Umbrellas*	New York	Viking	1994
Wolf, Bernard	*Homeless*	New York	Orchard Books	1995

Multicultural

Author	Title	Publisher City	Publisher Name	Date
Abeel, Samantha	*Reach for the Moon*	Duluth, MN	Pfeifer-Hamilton	1994
Ada, Alma Flor	*The Gold Coin*	New York	Aladdin Books	1991

Author	Title	Publisher City	Publisher Name	Date
Adams, Jeanie	Pigs and Honey	Adelaide, Australia	Omnibus Books	1989
Altman, Linda Jacobs	Amelia's Road	New York	Lee & Low	1993
Arnott, Kathleen	African Myths and Legends	New York	Oxford University Press	1990
Bachrach, Susan	Tell Them We Remember	Boston	Little Brown	1994
Baily, McLeish and Spearman	Gods and Men	New York	Oxford University Press	1993
Bang, Molly	The Paper Crane	New York	William Morrow	1987
Barber, Barbara E.	Saturday at the New You	New York	Lee & Low	1994
Barrett, Mary Brigin	Sing to the Stars	Boston	Little, Brown	1994
Beim, Lorraine Levey	Two Is a Team	New York	Harcourt Brace	1974
Birch, Cyril	Chinese Myths and Fantasies	New York	Oxford University Press	1987
Bontemps, A. & L. Hughes	Popo and Fifina	New York	Oxford University Press	1993
Brewster, Hugh	Anastasia's Album	New York	Hyperion Books for Children	1996
Briggs, Raymond	When the Wind Blows	New York	Schocken Books	1982
Caduto, Michael J. and J. Bruchac	Keepers of the Earth	Golden, CO	Fulcrum	1988
Cameron, Amy	The Stories Julian Tells	New York	Alfred A. Knopf	1981
Cannon, Janelle	Stellaluna	San Diego	Harcourt Brace	1993
Castaneda, Omar S.	Abuela's Weave	New York	Lee & Low	1993
Catalano, J. and S. Stotsky, eds	The Mexican Americans	New York	Chelsea House Publishers	1996
Chatterjee, Debjani	The Elephant-Headed God and Other Hindu Tales	New York	Oxford University Press	1992
Cisneros, Sandra	Hairs	New York	Alfred A. Knopf	1984
CityKids	CityKids Speak on Prejudice	New York	Random House	1994
Cohen, Barbara	Molly's Pilgrim	New York	William Morrow	1983
Collins, David R.	Casimir Pulaski	Gretna, LA	Gretna Publishing	1996
Corey, Dorothy	You Go Away	Niles, IL	Albert Whitman	1987
Dalal-Clayton, Diksha	The Adventures of Young Krishna, The Blue God of I	New York	Oxford University Press	1992
Dooley, Norah	Everybody Cooks Rice	New York	Scholastic	1991
Dorros, Arthur	Isla	New York	Dutton Children's Books	1995
Dorros, Arthur	Abuela	New York	Houghton Mifflin	1994
Farmer, Nancy	A Girl Named Disaster	New York	Orchard Books	1996
Feeney, Stephanie	Hawaii is a Rainbow	Honolulu	University of Hawaii Press	1985
Feeney, Stephanie	A is for Aloha	Honolulu	University of Hawaii Press	1980
Fern, Eugene	Pepito's Story	New York	Yarrow Press	1993
Filipovic, Zlata	Zlata's Diary	New York	Viking	1994
Fitzherbert, Sarah	My Dreaming Is the Christmas Bird	New South Wales	Ashton Scholastic	1989
Frank, Anne	Anne Frank's Tales from the Secret Annex	New York	Pocket Books	1949
Freedman, Russell	Indian Chiefs	New York	Holiday House	1987
Garg, Samidha and Jan Hardy	Racism (Global Issues Series)	Austin, TX	Raintree/Steck Vaughn	1997
Goble, Paul	Iktomi and the Ducks	New York	Orchard Book	1990
Grace, Patricia	Watercress Tuna and the Children of Champion Street	New York	Puffin Books	1985
Grimes, Nikki	Something on My Mind	New York	Puffin Books	1992
Haggerty, Mary Elizabeth	A Crack in the Wall	New York	Lee & Low	1993
Herold, Maggie Rugg	A Very Important Day	New York	Morrow Junior Books	1995

Author	Title	Publisher City	Publisher Name	Date
Hirschfelder, Arlene B.	*Happily May I Walk: American Indians*	New York	Scribner's	1986
Hoestlandt, Jo	*Star of Fear, Star of Hope*	New York	Walker and Company	1993
Howard, Elizabeth Fitzgerald	*Papa Tells Chita a Story*	New York	Simon & Schuster	1995
Hru, Dakari	*Joshua's Masai Mask*	New York	Lee & Low	1993
Hughes, L. & A. Bontemps	*The Pasteboard Bandit*	New York	Oxford University Press	1997
Hughes, Langston	*Black Misery*	New York	Oxford University Press	1994
Jenness, Aylette	*Families*	Boston	Houghton Mifflin	1990
Johnson-Feelings, Dianne, ed.	*The Best of The Brownies' Book*	New York	Oxford University Press	1996
Johnston, Tony	*Amber on the Mountain*	New York	Dial Books	1994
Jonas, An	*When You Were a Baby*	New York	Greenwillow	1991
Kahukiwa, Robyn	*Taniwha*	New York	Penguin Group	1986
Kempler, Susan	*A Man Can Be. . .*	New York	Human Sciences Press	1981
Kissinger, Katie	*All the Colors We Are*	St. Paul	Red Leaf Press	1994
Knight, Margy Burns	*Who Belongs Here?*	Gardiner, ME	Tilbury House	1993
Kraus, Robert	*Leo the Late Bloomer*	New York	Windmill Books	1971
Matiella, A.C.	*The Multicultural Caterpillar*	Marina, CA	Hampton-Brown	1971
Mendez, Consuelo	*Atariba & Niguayona*	San Francisco	Children's Book Press	1988
Mendez, Phil	*The Black Snowman*	New York	Scholastic	1989
Miller, William	*Zora Hurston and the Chinaberry Tree*	New York	Lee & Low	1994
Milne, Teddy	*Kids Who Have Made a Difference*	Northampton, MA	Pittenbruach Press	1989
Milord, Susan	*Hands Around the World*	Charlotte, VT	Williamson Publishing	1992
Mochizuki, Ken	*Baseball Saved Us*	New York	Lee & Low	1993
Moe, Barbara	*Coping With Bias Incidents*	New York	Rosen	1993
Mower, Nancy A.	*I Visit My Tutu and Grandma*	New York	Pr Pacifica	1984
Munsch, Robert	*Where is Gah-ning?*	Toronto	Annick Press	1994
Naidoo, Beverley	*Journey to Jo'burg*	New York	HarperCollins	1986
Nye, Naomi Shihab	*Sitti's Secret*	New York	Four Winds Press	1994
Orlando, Louise	*The Multicultural Game Book*	New York	Scholastic	1993
Ormerod, Jan	*Sunshine*	New York	Mulberry Books	1990
Ortiz, Simon	*The People Shall Continue*	San Francisco	Children's Book Press	1988
Paterson, Katherine	*The Sign of the Chrysanthemum*	New York	HarperCollins	1973
Polacco, Patricia	*I Can Hear the Sun*	New York	Philomel Books	1996
Ringgold, Faith	*Dinner at Aunt Connie's House*	New York	Hyperion Books for Children	1993
San Souci, Robert D.	*The Samurai's Daughter*	New York	Dial Books	1992
Seuss, Dr.	*The Sneetches and Other Stories*	New York	Random House	1961
Soto, Gary	*Living Up the Street*	New York	Dell Publishing	1985
Staples, Suzanne Fisher	*Shabanu*	New York	Random House	1989
Staples, Suzanne Fisher	*Haveli*	New York	Random House	1993
Tate, Eleanora E.	*The Secret of Gumbo Grove*	New York	Bantam Books	1988
Taylor, Mildred D.	*Let the Circle Be Unbroken*	New York	Puffin Books	1981
Taylor, Theodore	*The Cay*	New York	Avon Books	1959
Terzian, Alexandra	*The Kids' Multicultural Art Book*	Charlotte, VT	Williamson Publishing	1993
Torres, Leyla	*Saturday Sancocho*	New York	Farrar Straus and Giroux	1995
Turner, Robyn Montana	*Faith Ringgold*	New York	Little, Brown	1993

Author	Title	Publisher City	Publisher Name	Date
Utemorrah, Daisy	Do Not Go Around the Edges	Broome, Western Australia	Magabala Books Aboriginal Corp	1990
van der Rol, R. and V.R.	Anne Frank: Beyond the Diary	New York	Puffin Books	1993
Viola, Herman, ed.	American Indian Stories	Milwaukee	Raintree Publishers	1990
Watson, Jane Werner	The First Americans: Tribes of North America	New York	Pantheon Books	1980
Westridge Young Writer's	Kids Explore America's Hispanic Heritage	Santa Fe, NM	John Muir Publishers	1992
Williams, Shirley Anne	Working Cotton	San Diego	Harcourt Brace	1992
Williams, Vera B.	More, More, More, Said the Baby	New York	Greenwillow Books	1990
Woodson, Jacqueline	Melanin Sun	New York	The Blue Sky Press	1995
Yep, Laurence	The Serpent's Children	New York	Harper & Row	1984
Yep, Laurence	The Star Fisher	New York	Puffin Books	1991

Native-American

Author	Title	Publisher City	Publisher Name	Date
Bales, Carol A.	Kevin Cloud: Chippewa Boy in the City	New York	Contemporary Books	1972
Banks, Sarah	Remember My Name	Nimot, Co	Rinehart	1993
Baylor, Byrd	Hawk, I'm Your Brother	New York	Aladdin Books	1986
Baylor, Byrd	When Clay Sings	New York	Aladdin Books	1972
Baylor, Byrd	Everybody Needs a Rock	New York	Aladdin Books	1974
Bunting, Eve	Cheyenne Again	New York	Houghton Mifflin	1995
Caduto, Michael J. and J. Bruchac	Keepers of the Earth	Golden, CO	Fulcrum	1988
Cohen, Caron Lee	The Mud Pony	New York	Scholastic	1988
dePaola, Tomie	Legend of Indian Paintbrush	New York	Putnam	1988
Esbensen, Barbara Juster	The Great Buffalo Race	Boston	Little Brown	1994
Fradin, Dennis Brindell	Hiawatha	New York	Margaret K. McElderry Books	1992
Freedman, Russell	Indian Chiefs	New York	Holiday House	1987
Goble, Paul	Iktomi and the Ducks	New York	Orchard Book	1990
Gridley, Marion E.	American Indian Tribes	New York	Dodd, Mead & Co.	1974
Hirschfelder, Arlene B.	Happily May I Walk: American Indians	New York	Scribner's	1986
Jeffers, Susan	Brother Eagle, Sister Sky	New York	Dial Books	1991
Mendez, Consuelo	Atariba & Niguayona	San Francisco	Children's Book Press	1988
O'Dell, Scott & E. Hall	Thunder Rolling in the Mountains	New York	Dell Publishing	1992
Ortiz, Simon	The People Shall Continue	San Francisco	Children's Book Press	1988
Viola, Herman, ed.	American Indian Stories	Milwaukee	Raintree Publishers	1990
Waterton, Betty	A Salmon for Simon	New York	Groundwood Books	1996

Social Issues

Author	Title	Publisher City	Publisher Name	Date
Abeel, Samantha	Reach for the Moon	Duluth, MN	Pfeifer-Hamilton Publ.	1994
Ackerman, Karen	The Leaves in October	New York	Salamander	1995
Ada, Alma Flor	My Name is Maria Isabel	New York	Simon & Schuster	1995
Anzaldua, Gloria	Friends from the Other Side	San Francisco	Children's Book Press	1995
Ash, Maureen	The Story of the Women's Movement	Chicago	Children's Press	1989
Baily, McLeish and Spearman	Gods and Men	New York	Oxford University Press	1993

Author	Title	Publisher City	Publisher Name	Date
Bauman, Kurt	*The Hungry One*	New York	North-South	1993
Booker, Jean	*Ellen's Secret*			
Bosche, Susanne	*Jenny Lives with Eric and Martin*	London	Gay Men's Press	1983
Bunting, Eve	*Fly Away Home*	New York	Clarion Books	1991
Bunting, Eve	*Smoky Night*	San Diego	Harcourt Brace	1994
Bunting, Eve	*Cheyenne Again*	New York	Houghton Mifflin	1995
Cannon, Janelle	*Stellaluna*	San Diego	Harcourt Brace	1993
Chekhov, Anton	*Kashtanka*	New York	Gulliver Books	1995
Clifton, Lucille	*Don't You Remember?*	New York	E.P. Dutton	1973
Clifton, Lucille	*Everett Anderson's Friend*	New York	Henry Holt	1992
Clifton, Lucille	*Everett Anderson's Goodbye*	New York	Henry Holt	1983
Cohen, Barbara	*Molly's Pilgrim*	New York	William Morrow	1983
Coles, Robert	*The Story of Ruby Bridges*	New York	Scholastic	1995
Crofford, Emily	*A Place to Belong*	Minneapolis	Carolrhoda Books	1994
Curtis, Christopher Paul	*The Watsons Go to Birmingham—1963*	New York	Delacorte Press	1995
Dicks, Jan	*The House That Crack Built*	San Francisco	Chronicle Books	1992
DiSalvo-Ryan, DyAnne	*Uncle Willie and the Soup Kitchen*	New York	Morrow Junior Books	1991
Elwin, R. & M. Paulse	*Asha's Mums*	Toronto	The Woman's Press	1990
Evans, Douglas	*So What Do You Do*	New York	Front Street Press	1997
Ewing, Lynne	*Drive-By*	New York	Harper Collins	1996
Farber, Norma	*How Does it Feel to be Old?*	New York	E.P. Dutton	1990
Fast, Jonathan	*Newsies*		Disney	1992
Fleischman, Paul	*The Borning Room*	New York	HarperCollins	1991
Fox, John	*The Boys on the Rock*	New York	St. Martin's	1984
Fox, Mem	*Wilfrid Gordon McDonald Partridge*	Australia	Kane/Miller	1984
Fox, Paula	*Monkey Island*	New York	Orchard Books	1991
Fox, Paula	*The Slave Dancer*	New York	Dell Publishing	1973
Garg, Samidha & Jan Hardy	*Racism (Global Issues Series)*	Austin, TX	Raintree/Steck Vaughn	1997
Greenberg, Elliot Keith	*Erik is Homeless*	Minneapolis	Lerner Publications	1992
Guthrie, Donna	*A Rose for Abby*	Nashville	Abington Press	1988
Hamilton, Virginia	*The Magical Adventures of Pretty Pearl*	New York	Harper & Row	1983
Hathorn, Libby	*Way Home*	New York	Crown Publishers	1994
Holman, Felice	*The Wild Children*	New York	Puffin Books	1985
Johnson, Angela	*When I Am Old With You*	New York	Orchard Books	1990
Johnston, Tony	*Amber on the Mountain*	New York	Dial Books	1994
Jordon, Mary Kate	*Losing Uncle Tim*	Niles, IL	Albert Whitman & Co.	1989
Kissinger, Katie	*All the Colors We Are*	St. Paul	Red Leaf Press	1994
Knight, Margy Burns	*Who Belongs Here?*	Gardiner, ME	Tilbury House	1993
Koertge, Ron	*The Arizona Kid*	New York	Avon Books	1989
Kraus, Robert	*Leo the Late Bloomer*	New York	Windmill Books	1971
Kroloff, Rabbi Charles A.	*54 Ways You Can Help the Homeless*	Southport, CT	Hugh Lauter LevinAssoc.	1993
Lamb, Nancy	*Children Remember the Oklahoma City Bombing*	New York	Lothrop, Lee & Shepard	1996
Levine, Ellen	*Freedom's Children*	New York	Putnam	1993
Lorbiecki, Marybeth	*Just One Flick of a Finger*	New York	Dial Books	1996
Lowry, Lois	*The Giver*	Boston	Houghton Mifflin	1993
Lowry, Lois	*Number the Stars*	Boston	Houghton Mifflin	1989

Author	Title	Publisher City	Publisher Name	Date
Maruki, Tashi	*Hiroshima No Pika*	New York	Lathrop, Lee & Shepard	1980
Meltzer, Milton	*Underground Man*	New York	Harcourt Brace	1990
Mochizuki, Ken	*Heros*	New York	Lee & Low	1995
Near, Holly	*The Great Peace March*	New York	Henry Holt	1986
Newman, Leslea	*Gloria Goes to Gay Pride*	Boston	Allyson Wonderland	1991
Parks, Rosa	*I Am Rosa Parks*	New York	Dial Books	1997
Paterson, Katherine	*Lyddie*	New York	Puffin Books	1991
Paulsen, Gary	*Nightjohn*	New York	Bantam Doubleday Dell	1993
Paulsen, Gary	*The Crossing*	New York	Dell Publishing	1987
Polacco, Patricia	*Mrs. Katz and Tush*	New York	Bantam Books	1992
Polacco, Patricia	*Pink and Say*	New York	Philomel Books	1994
Polacco, Patricia	*Tikvah Means Hope*	New York	Doubleday	1996
Ringgold, Faith	*My Dreams of Martin Luther King*	New York	Crown Publishers	1995
Ringgold, Faith	*Aunt Harriet's Underground Railroad in the Sky*	New York	Crown Publishers	1992
Rylant, Cynthia	*I Had Seen Castles*	New York	Harcourt Brace	1993
Rylant, Cynthia	*An Angel for Solomon Singer*	New York	Orchard Books	1992
Skelton, Mora	*The Baritone Cat*	New York	Stoddart Kids	1996
Spohn, Kate	*Broken Umbrellas*	New York	Viking	1994
Staples, Suzanne Fisher	*Dangerous Skies*	New York	Farrar Strauss & Giroux	1996
Sullivan, George	*The Day the Women Got the Vote: A Photo History*	New York	Scholastic	1994
Tatsuharu, Kodama	*Shin's Tricycle*	New York	Walker and Company	1995
Terrell, Ruth	*A Kids Guide to How to Stop the Violence*	New York	Avon Books	1992
Tsuchiya, Yukio	*Faithful Elephants*	Boston	Houghton Mifflin	1988
Uchida, Yoshiko	*The Bracelet*	New York	Philomel Books	1993
Uchida, Yoshiko	*Journey to Topaz*	Berkeley	Creative Arts	1985
Varley, Susan	*Badger's Parting Gifts*	New York	Lothrop, Lee & Shepard	1984
Walker, Alice	*To Hell with Dying*	San Diego	Harcourt Brace	1993
White, R. and A.M. Cunningham	*My Own Story*	New York	Penguin Group	1991
Wild, Margaret	*Remember Me*	Niles, IL	Albert Whitman & Co.	1990
Wilhelm, Hans	*I'll Always Love You*	New York	Crown Publishers	1985
Willhoite, Michael	*Families: A Coloring Book*	Boston	Alyson	1991
Woodson, Jacqueline	*From the Notebooks of Melanin Sun*	New York	The Blue Sky Press	1995

Strong Girls

Author	Title	Publisher City	Publisher Name	Date
Ash, Maureen	*The Story of the Women's Movement*	Chicago	Children's Press	1989
Banks, Sarah	*Remember My Name*	Nimot, CO	Rinehart	1993
Baynton, Martin	*Jane and the Dragon*	Martinez, CA	Discovery Toys	1988
Behrens, June	*I Can Be a Truck Driver*	Chicago	Children's Press	1986
Browne, Anthony	*Piggybook*	New York	Alfred A. Knopf	1990
Coerr, Eleanor	*Sadako and the Thousand Paper Cranes*	New York	Dell Publishing	1977
Coerr, Eleanor	*Sadako*	New York	Putnam	1993
Cole, Babette	*Princess Smartypants*	New York	Putnam & Grosset	1986
Cole, Babette	*Prince Cinders*	New York	Putnam & Grosset	1987
Coleman, Evelyn	*White Socks Only*	Morton Grove, IL	Whitman	1996
Coles, Robert	*The Story of Ruby Bridges*	New York	Scholastic	1995
Emberley, Michael	*Ruby*	Boston	Little, Brown	1992

Author	Title	Publisher City	Publisher Name	Date
Fenner, Carol	*Yolanda's Genius*	New York	Aladdin Paperbacks	1995
Frank, Anne	*Anne Frank: The Diary of a Young Girl*	New York	Pocket Books	1952
French, Fiona	*Snow White in New York*	New York	Oxford University Press	1990
Hillesum, Etty	*An Interrupted Life*	New York	Pantheon Books	1981
Hoffman, Mary	*Amazing Grace*	New York	Magi Publishers	1995
Hoffman, Mary	*Boundless Grace*	New York	Dial Books	1995
Hopkinson, Deborah	*Sweet Clara and the Freedom Quilt*	New York	Alfred A. Knopf	1993
Innocenti, Roberto	*Rose Blanche*	Mankato, MN	Creative Education	1985
Jukes, Lila	*I'm a Girl!*	Boca Raton, FL	Cool Kids Press	1995
Kerr, M.E.	*Deliver us from Evie*	New York	HarperCollins	1994
Kherdian, David	*The Road from Home*	New York	Puffin Books	1979
Kogawa, Joy	*Itsuka*	New York	Doubleday	1992
Kogawa, Joy	*Obasan*	New York	Doubleday	1981
Krull, Kathleen	*Wilma Unlimited*	New York	Harcourt Brace	1996
Lyons, Mary E.	*Letters From A Slave Girl: The Story of Harriet Jacobs*	New York	Aladdin	1996
Martin, Rafe	*The Rough-Face Girl*	New York	Philomel Books	1992
Paterson, Katherine	*The Great Gilly Hopkins*	New York	Thomas Y. Crowell Co.	1978
Quindlen, Anna	*Happily Ever After*	New York	Viking	1997
Ringgold, Faith	*Tar Beach*	New York	Crown Publishers	1991
Rylant, Cynthia	*Missing May*	New York	Orchard Books	1992
Ryrie Brink, Carol	*Caddie Woodlawn*	New York	Aladdin	1990
Small, David	*Ruby Mae Has Something to Say*	New York	Crown Publishers	1992
Smalls-Hector, Irene	*Irene and the Big, Fine Nickel*	Boston	Little, Brown	1991
Staples, Suzanne Fisher	*Shabanu*	New York	Random House	1989
Staples, Suzanne Fisher	*Haveli*	New York	Random House	1993
Sullivan, George	*The Day the Women Got the Vote: A Photo History*	New York	Scholastic	1994
Taylor, Mildred D.	*The Road to Memphis*	New York	Puffin Books	1992
Voigt, Cynthia	*Dicey's Song*	New York	Fawcett Juniper Books	1982
Yolen, Jane	*The Devil's Arithmetic*	New York	Penguin Group	1988
Young, Ed	*Lon PoPo*	New York	Philomel Books	1989

Survival

Author	Title	Publisher City	Publisher Name	Date
Baillie, Allan	*Little Brother*	New York	Puffin Books	1985
Becerra de Jenkins, Lyll	*The Honorable Prison*	Nw York	Puffin Books	1989
Bishop, Claire Huchet	*Twenty and Ten*	New York	Puffin Books	1952
Buss, Fran Leeper	*Journey of the Sparrows*	New York	Dell Publishing	1991
Filipovic, Zlata	*Zlata's Diary*	New York	Viking	1994
Greenfeld, Howard	*The Hidden Children*	New York	Ticknor & Fields	1993
Kherdian, David	*The Road from Home*	New York	Puffin Books	1979
Kuper, Jack	*Child of the Holocaust*	New York	Signet Books	1967
Lewis, Elizabeth Foreman	*Young Fu of the Upper Yangtze*	New York	Dell Publishing	1932
Naidoo, Beverley	*Journey to Jo'burg*	New York	HarperCollins	1986
Orgel, Doris	*The Devil in Vienna*	New York	Puffin Books	1978
Raven, Margot	*Angels in the Dust*	New York	Bridge Water Books	1997
Reiss, Johanna	*The Upstairs Room*	New York	Bantam Books	1972
Tec, Nechama	*Dry Tears*	New York	Oxford University Press	1982

Author	Title	Publisher City	Publisher Name	Date
Turner, Glennette Tiley	*Running for our Lives*	New York	Holiday House	1994
Voigt, Cynthia	*Dicey's Song*	New York	Fawcett Juniper Books	1982
White, R. and A. M. Cunningham	*My Own Story*	New York	Penguin Group	1991
Wild, M. and Vivas, J.	*Let the Celebrations Begin!*	Norwood, South Australia	Omnibus Books	1991

Differently Abled

Author	Title	Publisher City	Publisher Name	Date
Aseltine, Lorraine	*I'm Deaf and it's Okay*	Niles, IL	Albert Whitman	1987
Berenstain, Stan and Jan	*The Berenstain Bears & The Wheelchair Commando*	New York	Random House	1993
Brown, Tricia	*Someone Special, Just Like You*	New York	Owlet	1995
Burnett, Frances Hodgson	*The Secret Garden*	New York	Random House	1993
Butts, Nancy	*Cheshire Moon*	New York	Front Street	1996
Carlson, Nancy	*Arnie and the New Kid*	New York	Puffin Books	1992
Carrick, Carol	*Melanie*	New York	Clarion Books	1996
Carter, Alden R. and Dan Young	*Big Brother Dustin*	Niles, IL	Albert Whitman	1997
Caseley, Judith	*Harry and Willy and Carrothead*	New York	Greenwillow	1991
Christopher, Matt and Karin Lidbeck	*Fighting Tackle (Sports Classics, vol. 49)*	Boston	Little, Brown	1996
Cowen-Letcher, Jane	*Mama Zooms*	New York	Scholastic	1996
Dinner, Sherry H.	*Nothing To Be Ashamed of: Growing Up With Mental Illness in Your Family*	New York	Lothrop Lee & Shepard	1989
Fassler, Joan	*Howie Helps Himself*	Niles, IL	Albert Whitman	1987
Fleming, Virginia	*Be Good to Eddie Lee*	New York	Philomel	1993
Foreman, Michael	*Seal Surfer*	New York	Harcourt Brace	1997
Johnson, Angela	*Humming Whispers*	New York	Orchard Books	1995
Joosse, Barbara M. and Gretchen Mayo	*Anna and the Cat Lady*	New York	HarperCollins	1992
Klein, Lee and Pam Mauseth	*Are There Stripes in Heaven?*	New York	Paulist	1994
Lakin, Patrica and Robert Steele	*Dad and Me in the Morning*	New York	Concepts Books	1994
Levin, Betty	*Away to Me, Moss!*	New York	Greenwillow Books	1994
Litchfield, Ada B. and Eleanor Mill	*A Button in Her Ear*	Niles, IL	Albert Whitman	1997
Moon, Nicola & Ale Ayliffe	*Lucy's Picture*	New York	Puffin Books	1995
O'Shaughnessy, Ellen	*Somebody Called Me a Retard Today . . . and My Heart Felt Sad*	New York	Walker & Co.	1992
Philbrick, Rodman	*Freak the Mighty*	New York	Scholastic	1993
Rabe, Berniece	*Where's Chimpy?*	Niles, IL	Albert Whitman	1991
Scott, Virginia M. and Patricia Crowe	*Belonging*	New York	Gallaudet University Press	1987
Shreve, Susan Richards	*The Gift of the Girls Who Couldn't Hear*	New York	William Morrow	1993
Springer, Nancy	*Colt*	New York	Puffin Books	1994
Susan, Gerardo	*Butterfly Boy*	New York	Boyds Mill Press	1997

Author	Title	Publisher City	Publisher Name	Date
Tamar, Erika	*Fair Game*	New York	Harcourt Brace	1993
Whelan, Gloria and Leslie Bowman	*Hannah (Stepping Stone Book)*	New York	Random House	1993
Wright, Betty Ren	*My Sister Is Different*	Austin, TX	Raintree/Steck Vaughn	1981

Professional Reference Books

Author	Title	Publisher City	Publisher Name	Date
AAUW	*How Schools Shortchange Girls*	New York	Marlowe & Co.	1995
Abbott, M. and B.J. Polk	*Celebrating Our Diversity Grade K-2*	Marina, CA	Hampton-Brown	1992
Ada, Alma Flor & Violet Harris L. Hopkins	*A Chorus of Cultures*	Marina, CA	Hampton-Brown	1994
Au, Kathryn	*Literacy Instruction in Multicultural Settings*	Fort Worth, TX	Harcourt Brace Jovanovich	1993
Barbieri, Maureen	*Sounds from the Heart, Learning to Listen to Girls*	Portsmouth, NH	Heinemann	1995
Barrs, Myra and Sue Pidgeon, eds.	*Reading the Difference*	York, ME	Stenhouse Publishers	1994
Bateson, Mary Catherine	*Peripheral Visions*	New York	HarperCollins	1994
Bauermeister, E. and J. Larsen and H. Smith	*500 Great Books by Women*	New York	Penguin Books	1994
Beane, J.A. and R.P. Lipka	*Self-Concept, Self-Esteem and the Curriculum*	New York	Teacher's College Press	1986
Belenky, M.F. et. al.	*Women's Ways of Knowing*	New York	Basic Books	1986
Bennett, Christine I.	*Comprehensive Multicultural Education, 3rd ed.*	Boston	Allyn & Bacon	1995
Berck, Judith	*No Place To Be—Voices of Homeless Children*	Boston	Houghton Mifflin	1992
Bettelheim, Bruno	*Surviving and Other Essays*	New York	Random House	1979
Bigelow, Bill, et. al. editors	*Rethinking our Classrooms: An Activist Education Journal*	Milwaukee, WI	Rethinking Schools, Inc.	1994
Bigelow, Bill, et. al. editors	*Rethinking our Classrooms: Teaching for Equity*	Milwaukee, WI	Rethinking Schools, Inc.	1994
Bingham, Mindy, et. al.	*Things Will be Different for My Daughter*	New York	Penguin Books	1995
Bishop, Rudine Sims	*Kaleidoscope: A Multicultural Booklist for Grades K–8*	Urbana, IL	NCTE	
Blais, Madeline	*In These Girls, Hope is a Muscle*	New York	Warner Books	1995
Blumenfield, Warren J. and D. Raymond	*Looking at Gay and Lesbian Life*	Boston	Beacon	1993
Breheney, Colleen and V. Mackrill and N. Grady	*Making Peace at Mayfield, A Whole School Approach*	Portsmouth, NH	Heinemann	1996
Caduto, Michael and Joseph Bruchac	*Keepers of the Earth: Native American Stories*	New York	Fulcrum	1989
Cammermeyer, Margarethe	*Serving in Silence*	Maryland	Prince Frederick	1996
Casey, Kathleen	*I Answer with My Life*	New York	Routledge	1993
Cazden, Coourtney	*Classroom Discourse*	Portsmouth, NH	Heinemann	1988
Chicago, Judy	*Holocaust Project*	New York	Penquin Group	1993
Cisneros, Sandra	*The House on Mango Street*	New York	Knopf	1994
Crawford, Susan Hoy	*Beyond Dolls and Guns*	Portsmouth, NH	Hainemann	1996

Author	Title	Publisher City	Publisher Name	Date
Csikszentmihalyi, Mihaly	Finding Flow	New York	HarperCollins	1997
Csikszentmihalyi, Mihaly	Creativity	New York	HarperCollins	1996
Csikszentmihalyi, Mihaly	Flow: The Psychology of Optimal Experience	New York	Harper & Row	1990
Daniels, Harvey, A. ed.	Not Only English	Urbana, IL	NCTE	1990
Day, Frances Ann	Multicultural Voices in Contemporary Literature: A Resource for Teachers	Portsmouth, NH	Heinemann	1994
Day, Frances	Multicultural Voices	Portsmouth, NH	Heinemann	1994
Debold, E. et. al.	Mother Daughter Revolution	Reading, MA	Addison-Wesley	1993
Delpit, Lisa	Other People's Children	New York	The New Press	1995
Derman-Sparks, Louise	Other People's Children Anti-Bias Curriculum: Tools for Empowering Young Children	New York	NAEYC	1969
di Leonardo, Micaela	Gender at the Crossroads	Berkeley, CA	University of Calif. Press	1991
Dillard, Annie	An American Childhood	New York	HarperCollins	1988
Duberman, Vicinus and Chauncey, eds.	Hidden From History	New York	NAL/Penguin	1989
Edelskky, Carole	With Literacy and Justice for All	London	The Falmer Press	1991
Edelsky, Carole Altwerger, and B. Flores	Whole Language: What's the Difference?	Portsmouth, NH	Heinemann	1991
Enloe, Walter and Ken Smith eds.	Linking Through Diversity: Practical Classroom Activities	Marina, CA	Hampton-Brown	1993
Ernst, Karen	Picturing Learning	Portsmouth, NH	Heinemann	1994
Farr, Marcia and Harvey Daniels	Language Diversity and Writing Instruction	New York	ERIC Clearinghouse	1986
Firestone, Shulamith	The Dialectic of Sex	New York	William Morrow	1970
Frankl, Victor E.	Psychotherapy and Existentialism	New York	Simon & Schuster	1976
Freeman, David and Yvonne	Between Worlds	Portsmouth, NH	Heinemann	1994
Freeman, Yvonne and David	Whole Language for Second Language Learners	Portsmouth, NH	Heinemann	1992
Freeman, David and Yvonne	Teaching Reading & Writing in Spanish in the Bilingual Class	Portsmouth, NH	Heinemann	1997
Gilbert, Pam & Sandra Taylor	Fashioning the Femine	North Sydney, Australia	Allen & Unwin	1991
Gilligan, Carol	In a Different Voice	Cambridge, MA	Harvard University Press	1982
Gilligan, Carol	Mapping the Moral Domain	Cambridge, MA	Harvard University Press	1988
Gilligan, Carol	Making Connections	Cambridge, MA	Harvard University Press	1990
Gilyard, Keith	Voices of the Self	Detroit, MI	Wayne State University	1991
Goleman, Daniel	Emotional Intelligence	New York	Bantam Books	1995
Goodman, Y.M. and A.M. Marek	Retrospective Miscue Analysis	Katonah, NY	Richard C. Owens	1996
Goodman, Yetta M.	Notes from a Kid Watcher	Portsmouth, NH	Heinemann	1996
Graves, Donald	A Fresh Look at Writing	Portsmouth, NH	Heinemann	1994
Gunner, Elizabeth	A Handbook for Teaching African Literature	Portsmouth, NH	Heinemann	1984
Harbeck, Karen M., ed.	Coming Out of the Classroom Closet	New York	Harrington Park Press	1992

Author	Title	Publisher City	Publisher Name	Date
Harris, Violet J., ed.	*Teaching Multicultural Literature in Grades K-8*	Marina, CA	Hampton-Brown	1996
Heilbrun, Carolyn G.	*Hamlet's Mother and Other Women*	New York	Ballantine Books	1990
Helgesen, Sally	*The Female Advantage*	New York	Doubleday	1990
Herdt, Gilbert	*Gay and Lesbian Youth*	New York	Harrington Park	1989
Herdt, Gilbert and A. Boxer	*Children of Horizons*	Boston	Beacon	1993
Hiebert, Elfrieda	*Literacy for a Diverse Society*	New York	Teachers College Press	1991
Hillesum, Etty	*An Interrupted Life*	New York	Pantheon Books	1981
Hooks, Bell	*Yearning*	Boston	South End Press	1990
Hooks, Bell	*Outlaw Culture*	New York	Routledge	1994
Hooks, Bell	*A Woman's Mourning Song*	New York	Harlem River Press	1993
Hooks, Bell	*Talking Back*	Boston	South End Press	1989
Hooks, Bell	*Teaching to Transgress*	New York	Routledge	1994
Hubbard, Ruth Shagoury	*Workshop of the Possible*	York, ME	Stenhouse Publishers	1996
Hubert, C. Mark and S. Toten	*Social Issues in the English Classroom*	Urbana, IL	NCTE	1992
Jennings, Kevin, ed.	*One Teacher in Ten*	Boston	Alyson	1994
Kostlowitz, Alex	*There Are No Children Here*	New York	Bantam Doubleday	1993
Kovner, Abba	*Scrolls of Fire*	Jerusalem	Keter Publishing House	1981
Kozol, Jonathon	*Rachel and Her Children*	New York	Crown Publishers	1988
Krall, Florence T.	*Ecotone*	Albany, NY	State University of NY Press	1994
Kucer, S.B., C. Silva-E, Delgado-LaRocco	*Curricular Conversations*	York, ME	Stenhouse Publishers	1995
Kuklin, Susan	*Speaking Out: Teenagers Take on Race, Sex, and Identity*	New York	G.P. Putnam's Sons	1993
Lanzmann, Claude	*Shoa: The Complete Text*	New York	Pantheon Books	1995
Lawrence-Lightfoot, Sara	*I've Known Rivers*	Reading, MA	Addison-Wesley	1994
Lee, Enid	*Letters to Marcia: A Teacher's Guide to Anti-Racist Education*	New York	Cross Cultural Communication	1986
Leitner, Isabella	*Saving the Fragments*	New York	New American Library	1986
Lerner, Gerda	*Teaching Women's History*	Washington, D.C.	American Historical Assoc.	1981
Levin, Diane E.	*Teaching Young Children in Violent Times*	New York	New Society Press	1994
Loewen, James	*Lies My Teacher Told Me*	New York	New Press	1996
Lurie, Alison	*Don't Tell the Grown-ups*	Boston	Little Brown & Co.	1990
Macy, Sue	*Winning Ways*	New York	Henry Holt	1996
Maher, Frances and Mary Kay Thompson Tetreault	*The Feminist Classroom*	New York	HarperCollins	1994
Manning, Maryann, Manning, Gary and Roberta Long	*Theme Immersion*	Portsmouth, NH	Heinemann	1994
Miller, Alice	*The Untouched Key*	New York	Doubleday	1990
Murray, Denise	*Diversity as Resource*	Alexandria, VA	TESOL	1992
National Coalition of Education Activists	*Fighting Back Against Violence*	New York	NCEA	1994
Nelson, Mariah Burton	*The Stronger Women Get, the More Men Love Football*	New York	Avon Books	1994

Author	Title	Publisher City	Publisher Name	Date
Nieto, Sonia	*Affirming Diversity*	New York	Longman Publishing	1992
O'Connor, Karen	*Homeless Children*	California	Lucent Books	1989
O'Neil, Teresa	*The Homeless*	California	Greenhaven Press	1990
O'Reilley, M.R.	*The Peaceable Classroom*	Portsmouth, NH	Boynton/Cook	1993
Orenstein, Peggy	*SchoolGirls*	New York	Doubleday	1994
Osborne, K. and W. Spurlin, eds.	*Reclaiming the Heartland*	Minneapolis	University of Minnesota Press	1996
Osen, Lynn	*Women in Mathematics*	Cambridge, MA	MIT Press	1974
Paley, Vivian Gussin	*You Can't Say You Can't Play*	Cambridge	Harvard University Press	1993
Peregoy, S.F. and O.F. Boyle	*Reading, Writing, and Learning in ESL*	White Plains, NY	Longman Publishing	1993
Peterson, Bob	*Teachers and Parents: The Milwaukee Experience*	Milwaukee	City College	1991
Pipher, Mary	*Reviving Ophelia*	New York	Ballantine Books	1994
Pipher, Mary	*The Shelter of Each Other*	New York	Ballantine Books	1997
Rawlins, William K.	*Friendship Matters*	New York	Walter de Gruyter	1992
Remafedi, Gary	*Death by Denial*	Boston	Alyson Publications	1994
Ribbens, Jane	*Mothers and their Children*	London	Sage Publications	1994
Rigg, Pat and Virginia Allen, ed.	*When They Don't All Speak English*	Urbana, IL	NCTE	1989
Rochman, Hazel	*Against the Borders*	Chicago	American Library Assoc.	1993
Rose, Mike	*Lives on the Boundary*	New York	Penguin Books	1989
Rose, Mike	*Possible Lives*	New York	Penguin Books	1995
Roser, N.L. & Martinez, M.G.	*Book Talk and Beyond*	Newark, DE	IRA	1995
Sadker, Myra & David	*Failing at Fairness*	New York	Charles Scribner's Sons	1994
San Souci, R.D.	*Cut from the Same Cloth*	New York	Philomel Books	1993
Schniedewind, Nancy and Ellen Davidson	*Cooperative: Learning, Cooperative Lives*	New York	Wm. C. Brown Co.	1987
Schniedewind, Nancy and Elllen Davidson	*Open Minds to Equality: A Sourcebook of Learning Activities*	Englewood Cliffs, NJ	Prentice Hall	1983
Segal, Lore	*Other People's Houses*	New York	Fawcett Crest	1958
Seligman, Martin E.	*The Optimistic Child*	New York	Houghton Mifflin	1995
Siegal, Aranka	*Upon the Head of a Goat*	New York	Farrar Straus amd Giroux	1981
Shannon, Patrick	*Becoming Political: Readings and Writings*	Portsmouth, NH	Heinemann	1992
Short, K. and C. Burke	*Creating Curriculum*	Portsmouth, NH	Heinemann	1991
Short, Kathy, Harsten, Jerome and Carolyn Burke	*Creating Classrooms for Authors and Inquirers*	Portsmouth, NH	Heinemann	1996
Solsken, J.W.	*Literacy, Gender and Work*	Norwood, NJ	Ablex Publ.	1993
Spiegelman, Art	*Maus II: And Here My Troubles Began*	New York	Pantheon Books	1991
Spiegelman, Art	*Maus*	New York	Pantheon Books	1986
Studkey, J.E.	*The Violence of Literacy*	Portsmouth, NH	Boynton-Cook	1991
Swann, Joan	*Girls, Boys, and Language*	Oxford, UK	Blackwell Publishers	1992
Tannen, Deborah	*That's Not What I Meant*	New York	Ballantine Books	1986
Tannen, Deborah	*Talking from 9 to 5*	New York	William Morrow	1994
Tannen, Deborah, ed.	*Gender and Conversational Interaction*	New York	Oxford University Press	1993
Tannen, Deborah, ed.	*Framing in Discourse*	New York	Oxford University Press	1993
Tannen, Deborah	*Gender and Discourse*	New York	Oxford University Press	1994

Author	Title	Publisher City	Publisher Name	Date
Tannen, Deborah	*Talking Voices*	New York	Cambridge Univesity Press	1989
Tannen, Deborah	*You Just Don't Understand*	New York	Ballantine Books	1990
Taylor, Denny	*Toxic Literacies Exposing the Injustice of Bureaucratic Text*	Portsmouth, NH	Heinemann	1996
Thorne, Barrie	*Gender Play*	New Brunswick, NH	Rutgers University Press	1994
United Nations	*The World's Women 1995*	New York	United Nations	1995
Villanueva, Victor	*Bootstraps*	Urbana, IL	NCTE	1993
Wade, Rahima Carol	*Joining Hands from Personal to Planetary Friendship*	Marina, CA	Hampton-Brown	1991
Walling, Donovan, ed.	*Open Lives Safe Schools*	Bloomington, IL	Phi Delta Kappa	1996
Whaley, L and L. Dodge	*Weaving in the Women*	Portsmouth, NH	Boynton/Cook	1993
Whiten, Phyllis	*Sketching Stories, Stretching Minds*	Portsmouth, NH	Heinemann	1996
Whitmore, K.F. and C.G. Crowell	*Inventing a Classroom*	York, ME	Stenhouse Publishers	1994
Wiesel, Elie	*Night/Dawn/Day*	New York	Aronson	1995
Williams, Gregory Howard	*Life on the Color Line: The True Story of a White Boy*	New York	Plume	1996
Young, Iris Marion	*Justice and the Politics of Difference*	Princeton, NJ	Princeton University Press	1990

F

Other Resources for Teaching for Social Justice

Akwesasne Notes Newspaper, Mohawk Nation: Rooseveltown, NY 13693

Alternatives, P.O. Box 1050, Amherst, MA 01004-1050, (413) 546-4523

American Indian Library Association, Atlanta, GA

American Indian Newsletter, New Mexico State University, Box 30006, Las Cruces, NM 88003-0006

Amnesty International USA, 53 West Jackson, Rm. 1162, Chicago, IL 60604, (312) 427-2060

Anti-Defamation League, 309 W. Washington Street, Suite 78, Chicago, IL 60606-3296, (312) 782-5080

Center for Applied Linguistics, 1118 22nd Street, NW, Washington, DC 20037, (202) 429-9292

Children's Book Press, 1461 Ninth Avenue, San Francisco, CA 94122

Equity Institute, 48 North Pleasant St., Amherst, MA 01002, (413) 256-0271

Gay and Lesbian Alliance Against Defamation/LA, 8455 Beverly Blvd., Suite 305, Los Angeles, CA 90048, (213) 658-6775

Homebase, 870 Market St., Suite 1228, San Francisco, CA 94102-2907, (415) 788-7961

Indian Historian Press, 1493 Masonic Avenue, San Francisco, CA 94117

Interracial Books for Children Bulletin, New York: CIBC (8 issues per year)

Multicultural Education Curriculum: Learning Activities for 7th & 8th Grade Social Studies Classes, NYC Board of Education, 52 Chambers St., Rm. 311, NY, NY, 10007

National Association for the Education of Young Children, Washington, DC

National Association of State Coordinators for the Education of Homeless Children and Youth

National Coalition for the Homeless, 1612 K St., NW, Suite 1004, Washington, DC 20006-2802, (202) 775-1322

National Law Center on Homelessness & Poverty, 918 F St., NW, Suite 412, Washington, DC 20004-1406, (202) 638-2535

Native American Authors Distribution Project, The Greenfield Review Press, 2 Middle Grove Road, P.O. Box 308, Greenfield Center, NY 12833

OYATE, 2702 Mathews Street, Berkeley, CA 94702

Rethinking Schools, An Urban Educational Journal, 1001 E. Keefe Ave., Milwaukee, WI 53212

School Voices, 115 W. 28th St., Suite 3-R, New York, NY

Cooperative Children's Book Center, University of Wisconsin-Madison: Wisconsin Department of Public Instruction,

Task Force on Lesbian and Gay Issues, 50 California Street, San Francisco, CA 94111-4696, (415) 772-4300

The Campaign to End Homophobia, P.O. Box 438316, Chicago, IL 60643-8316

The Council on Interracial Books for Children (CIBC), 1841 Broadway, NY, NY 10023

The National Center for Research on Cultural Diversity and Second Language Learning (NCRCDSLL), 1118 22nd Street, NW, Washington, DC 20037, (202) 429-9292

Theytus Books, Ltd., Box 218, Penticton, British Columbia V2A 6K3, Canada

Third World Press, P.O. Box 730, Chicago, IL 60619

Townley, Charles, American Indian Libraries Newsletter, New Mexico: New Mexico State University

UNICEF

Unified School District Support Services for Gay and Lesbian Youth, 1512 Golden Gate Avenue, San Francisco, CA 94115 (415) 749-3424

U.S. Department of Education, 600 Independence Ave. SW, Room 4168, Washington, DC 20202-8240, (202) 401-0590

Women's Educational Media, 2180 Bryant Street, Suite 203, San Francisco, CA 94110

Youths AIDS Project. Adolescent Health Program, Box 721, University of Minnesota, Hospital and Clinic, Harvard Street at East River Road, Minneapolis, Minnesota 55455, (612) 626-2220

Books and Articles

Adoff, Arnold. *All the Colors of the Race*. New York, NY: Lothrop Lee and Shepard Books, 1982

Affording Equal Opportunity to Gay and Lesbian Students Through Teaching and Counseling. National Education Association, Human and Civil Rights, 1201 Sixteenth St., NW, Washington, DC 20036 (1993)

Altman, Susan. *Extraordinary Black Americans from Colonial to Contemporary Times*. Chicago, IL: Children's Press, 1989

Angell, Carole S. *Celebrations Around the World: A Multicultural Handbook*. Golden, CO: Fulcrum Publishing (800) 992-2908.

August, D. and L. Pease-Alvarez. *Attributes of Effective Programs and Classrooms Serving English Language Learners*. Center for Applied Linguistics, 1118 22nd Street, NW, Washington, DC 20037, (202) 429-9292

Austin, Mary C. *Promoting World Understanding Through Literature, K-8*. Littleton, CO: Libraries Unlimited, 1983.

Baruth, Leroy G. *Multicultural Education of Children and Adolescents*. Boston, MA: Allyn and Bacon, 1992.

Bass, Ellen and Kate Kauffman. *Free Your Mind: The Book for Gay, Lesbian and Bisexual Youth and Their Allies*. New York: Harper Perennial, 1996.

Bergstrom, Sage and Lawrence Cruz, eds. *Counseling Lesbian and Gay Male Youth: Their Special Lives/Special Needs*. National Network of Runaway and Youth Services, 1983.

Bielke, Patricia F. and Frank J. Sciara. *Selecting Materials for and About Hispanic and East Asian Children and Young People*. Shoe String Press, 1986.

Celebrate America's Diversity: Holidays, Festivals and Historical Events Celebrated and Recognized by African Americans, American Indians, Asian/Pacific Islanders and Latinos.

Chase, Josephine, *Multicultural Spoken Here: Discovering America's People Through Language Arts and Library Skills*. Santa Monica, CA: Goodyear Publishing Co., 1979.

Chicago: Middleton Education Resources, 1993.

Council on Interracial Books for Children, *Selecting Bias-Free Textbooks and Storybooks*. New York: The Council.

Council on Interracial Books for Children. *Unlearning Indian Stereotypes: A Teaching Unit for Elementary Teachers and Children's Librarians*. New York: The Council, 1977.

Cox, Rita. *Multicultural Programming*. Ottawa, Ontario: Canadian Library Association, 1989.

Darby, Jean. *Martin Luther King, Jr.* Minneapolis, MN: Lerner Publication Co., 1990.

Derman-Sparks, Louise and C. Higa and B. Sparks. *Children, Race and Racism: How Race Awareness Develops*. Washington, DC: National Association for the Education of Young Children, 1980.

Derman-Sparks, Louise and Gutierrez and Phillips. *Teaching Young Children to Resist Bias*. Washington DC: National Association for the Education of Young Children, 1989.

Derman-Sparks, Louise. *How Well are We Nurturing Racial and Ethnic Diversity?* CSAC Review, 4 (2), 1985.

Derman-Sparks, Louise. *Anti-bias Curriculum: Tools for Empowering Young Children.* Washington DC: National Association for the Education of Young Children, 1989.

Different Faces: Growing Up With Books in a Multicultural Society. London: Pluto, 1988.

Due, Linnea. *Joining the Tribe: Growing Up Gay in the 90's.* New York: Bantam Doubleday Dell Publishing Group, 1995.

Gordon, Lenore. "What Do We Say When We Hear 'Faggot'?" *Rethinking Schools*, May/June 1992.

Gough, Cal and Ellen Greenblatt, eds. *Gay and Lesbian Library Service.* Jefferson, NC: McFarland and Company, Inc., 1990.

Grant, Carl A. and Christine E. Sleet. *Turning on Learning: Five Approaches for Multicultural Teaching Plans for Race, Class, Gender, and Disability.* Columbus, OH: Merrill Publishing Co., 1989.

Griffin, Louise. *Multi-Ethnic Books for Young Children.* Washington D.C.: National Association for the Education of Young Children, 1971.

Griswold, Vera Jo and Judith Starke. *Multi-Cultural Art Projects.* Denver, CO: Love, 1980.

Harris, Jacqueline L. *Martin Luther King, Jr.* New York, NY: F. Watts, 1983.

Hayden, Carla D. ed. *Venture Into Cultures: A Resource Book of Multicultural Materials and Programs* Chicago, IL: American Library Association, 1992.

Hidalgo, Hilda, Twain L. Peterson, and Natalie J. Woodman eds. *Lesbian and Gay Issues: A Resource Manual for Social Workers.* Silver Spring, MD: National Association of Social Workers, 1980.

Johnson, Dianne. *Telling Tales: The Pedagogy and Promise of African American Literature for Youth.* New York, NY: Greenwood, 1990.

Kappa Delta Pi. *Star Teachers of Children in Poverty.* Kappa Delta Pi, P.O. Box A, 1601 W. State Street, West Lafayette, IN 47906-0576 (317) 743-1705.

Klein, Gillian. *Reading into Racism: Bias in Children's Literature and Learning Materials.* London: Routledge, 1985.

Kosof, Anna. *Jesse Jackson.* New York, NY: F. Watts, 1987.

Kruse, Ginny Moore and Kathleen T. Horning. *By and About People of Color.* Madison, WI: Cooperative Children's Book Center, University of Wisconsin-Madison, Wisconsin Department of Public Instruction, 1991.

Lachmann, Lyn Miller. *Our Family, Our Friends, Our World: An Annotated Guide to Significant Multicultural Books for Children and Teenagers.* New Providence, NJ: R.R. Bowker, 1992.

Lindgren, Merri, ed. *The Multicolored Mirror: Cultural Substance in Literature for Children and Young Adults.* Fort Atkinson, WI: Highsmith Press, 1991.

Lowe, Robert, Bob Peterson and Rita Tenorio. *Rethinking Schools: An Urban Educational Journal.* Milwaukee, WI.

Lowery, Linda. *Martin Luther King Day.* Minneapolis, MN: Carolrhoda Books, 1987.

MacCann, Donnarae and Gloria Woodard, eds. *The Black American in Books for Children: Readings in Racism.* Metuchen, NJ: Scarecrow Press, 1972.

Mallett, Jerry J. *World Folktales: A Multicultural Approach to Whole Language.* Fort Atkinson, WS: Alleyside Press, 1994.

Massey, Ian. *More Than Skin Deep: Developing Anti-Racist Multicultural Education in Schools.* London: Hodder and Sloughton, 1991.

McCracken, J. *Valuing Diversity: The Primary Years.* Washington DC: National Association for the Education of Young Children,1993.

McDonald, Helen B and Audrey Steinborn. *Homosexuality: A Practical Guide to Counseling Lesbians, Gay Men, and Their Families.* New York: Continuum Publications, 1990.

McKissack, Pat. *Frederick Douglass the Black Lion.* Chicago, IL: Children's Press, 1987.

McKissack, Psat. *Paul Laurence Dunbar, A Poet to Remember.* Chicago, IL: Childre's Press, 1984.

McKissack, Pat. *Mary McLeod Bethune: A Great American Educator*. Chicago, IL: Children's Press, 1985.

Miller, Douglas T. *Frederick Douglass and the Fight for Freedom*. New York, NY: Facts on File, 1988.

Multicultural Teaching: A Handbook of Activities, Information and Resources. Boston, MA: Allyn and Bacon, 1990.

Myers, Walter Dean. *Now Is Your Time*. New York, NY: HarperCollins Publishers, 1991.

Neugebauer, B., ed. *Alike and Different: Exploring our Humanity with Young Children*. Washington DC: National Association for the Education of Young Children, 1992.

Nichols, Margaret S. *Multicultural Bibliography for Preschool Through Second Grade: In the Areas of Black, Spanish Speaking, Asian American and Native American Cultures*. Stanford, CA: Multicultural Resources, 1972.

Ortiz, Victoria. *Sojourner Truth, A Self-Made Woman*. Philadelphia, PA: Lippincott, 1974.

Patterson, Lillie. *Martin Luther King, Jr.: Man of Peace*. New York, NY: Dell Publishing Co., 1969.

Porter, A.P., *Kwanzaa*. Minneapolis, MN: Carolrhoda Books, 1991.

Quint, Sharon. *Schooling Homeless Children: A Working Model for America's Public Schools*. New York: Teachers College Press, 1994.

Preiswerk, Roy, ed. *The Slant of the Pen: Racism in Children's Books*. Geneva, Switzerland: World Council of Churches, 1988.

Racism and Sexism in Children's Books. Writers and Readers. New York, NY: Council on Interracial Books for Children, 1979.

Ramses, Patricia. *Making Friends at School*, 1997.

Ramses, Patricia. *Multicultural Education for Young Children*, 1978.

Ramses, Patricia. *Teaching and Learning in a Diverse World*.

Riehl, Peggy. *Five Ways to Analyze Classrooms for an Anti-Bias Approach. English*, May 23, 1997.

Rollock, Barbara. *Black Authors and Illustrators for Children's Books: A Biographical Dictionary*. New York, NY: Garland, 1988.

Savin-Williams, Ritch C. *Gay and Lesbian Youth: Expressions of Identity*. New York: Hemisphere Pub. Corp. 1990.

Schloredt, Valarie. *Martin Luther King, Jr.: America's Great Nonviolent Leader in the Struggle for Human Rights*. Milwaukee, MN: G. Stevens, 1988.

Schnider, Margaret S. *Often Invisible: Counseling Gay and Lesbian Youth*. Central Toronto, Ontario: Toronto Youth Services, 27 Carilton St., 1988.

Schofield, R.T. *Celebrating Our Differences*. 1985.

Schubert, Barbara. *Black History: A Book of Culturally Based Activities for K-6 Children*. San Jose, CA: Reflections and Images, 1977.

Shinn, Marybeth and Beth Weitzman. *Homelessness in America*. Washington DC: National Coalition for the Homeless, 1996.

Short, D. *Integrating Language and Culture in Middle School American History Classes*. Center for Applied Linguistics, 1118 22nd Street, NW, Washington, DC 20037, (202) 429-9292.

Simes, Rudine. *Shadow and Substance: Afro-American Experience in Contemporary Children's Fiction*. Urbana, IL: National Council of Teachers of English, 1982.

Slapin, Beverly and Doris Seale. *Books Without Bias: Through Indian Eyes*. Berkeley, CA: OYATE, 1988.

Snead Howard. *The Afro-Americans*. New York, NY: Chelsea House Publishers, 1989.

Stull, Edith Gilbert. *Unsung Black Americans*. New York, NY: Grossett & Dunlap, 1971.

Teaching Tolerance. 400 Washington Avenue, Montgomery, AL 36104 (Fax: 334-264-3121).

Unks, Gerald, ed. *The Gay Teen: Educational Practice and Theory for Lesbian, Gay, and Bisexual Adolescents*. New York: Routledge, 1995.

Williams, Helen E. *Books by African-American Authors and Illustrators for Children and Young Adults*. Chicago, IL: American Library Association, 1991.

Woog, Dan. *Schools Out: The Impact of Gay and Lesbian Issues on America's Schools*. Boston, MA: Alyson Publications Inc., 1995.

Music

American Indian Music: Canyon Records, 4143 North 16th Street, Phoenix, AZ 85016.

Belkin, Allen, ed. *Songs for Social Justice*. 1994.

UNICEF. *A Children's Chorus: Celebrating the 30th Anniversary of the Universal Declaration of the Rights of the Child*. New York: E.P. Dutton, 1989.

Other

"Struggle for Equality: The Lesbian and Gay Community," *School Voices*. 115 W. 28th St., Suite 3-R, New York, NY: (212) 643-8490.

A Guide to Leading Introductory Workshops on Homophobia. The Campaign to End Homophobia, P.O. Box 819, Cambridge, MA 02139, 1990.

Bahr, Mary. *The Memory Box*. New York: Albert Whitman & Co., 1995.

DeAndrade, Kim. "Facts, Feelings and Attitudes About Homosexuality." *FLEducator*, Winter 1992/1993.

Edelsky, Carole. *Let's Talk Theory*, an audio tape. Network Communications, P.O. Box 219, High Ridge, MO 63049, (314) 677-1912.

Establishing Classroom Rules Against Namecalling. Equity Institute, 48 North Pleasant St., Amherst, MA 01002, (413) 256-0271.

Gordon, Leonate, "Homophobia and Education: How to Deal with Name-Calling and Countering Homophobia: A Lesson Plan," Interracial Books for Children Bulletin, Vol. 14, No. 3 & 4, 1983.

Gordon, Lynn. *52 Ways to Make a Difference*. Illustrated cards. San Francisco: Chronicle Books.

Harriet the Spy. Film. Paramount, 1996.

Hoffman, Marvin, "Teaching Torch Song: *Gay Literature in the Classroom*, National Council of Teachers of English, *English Journal*, September, 1993.

Indigenous Heroes Poster. OYATE, 1996.

Iroqrafts, RR#2, Ohsweken, Ontario, Canada NOA 1MO.

It's Elementary: Teaching Gay Issues in School. Film, New Day Films, Dept. FL, 22-D Hollywood Ave., Hohokus, NJ 07423.

Lipkin, Arthur. *Looking at Gay and Lesbian Literature*. Cambridge, MA: Harvard Graduate School of Education, 1992.

Lipkin, Arthur, *Strategies for the Teacher: Using Gay/Lesbian-Related Materials in the Classroom*. Cambridge, MA: Harvard Graduate School of Education, 1992.

Lipkin, Arthur. *The History and Nature of Homosexuality*. Cambridge, MA: Harvard Graduate School of Education, 1992.

Lipkin, Arthur. *The Stonewall Riots and the History of Gays and Lesbians in the United States*. Cambridge, MA: Harvard Graduate School of Education, 1992.

Million Man March. Film.

National Theater of the Performing Arts, Ltd. information on national touring companies, class and school fieldtrips, educational, cultural, bilingual, live theater programs.

Pocahontas. Film, Disney, 1995.

Reach Every Child, a list of over 2000 resources for teachers and students. 642 Chaparel, Mira Lorna, CA 91762.

Saavedra, Elizabeth. *Transforming Whole Language: Beyond Project Diversity*. Audio tape. Network Communications, P.O. Box 219, High Ridge, MO 63049.

Sexual Orientation: Reading Between the Labels. NEWIST/CESA#7, IS 1110, University of Wisconsin, Green Bay, WI, 54311.

Shanley, Mary Kay. *The Memory Box: Gathering the Keepsakes of the Heart*. New York: Sta Kris, 1996.

Schindler's List. Film, Universal, 1993.

Sports Illustrated. Kids' cards.

Sticks, Stones and Stereotypes. Videotape. Equity Institute, 48 North Pleasant St., Amherst, MA 01002. (413) 256-0271.

Meeting the Challenge of Teaching Linguistically Diverse Students. Video series. The National
   Center for Research on Cultural Diversity and Second Language Learning, Center for
   Applied Linguistics, 1118 22nd Street, NW, Washington, DC 20037.
Western Trading Post, P.O. Box 9070, 32 Broadway, Denver, CO 80209.

Web Sites

http://i-site.on.ca/booknook/index.html — Book Nook

http://www.bookwire.com/links/readingroom/echildbooks.htm — BookWire Electronic Children's Book Index

http://www.afn.org/~afn15301/drseuss.html — Cyber-Seuss

http://www.disney.com/DisneyBooks/ — Disney's Amazing Book Factory!

http://www.womedia.org — Educational media about women

http://ipl.sils.umich.edu/youth/HomePage.html — Internet Public Library Youth Division

www.cyfc.umn.edu/diversity/gay/secret.html — Lesbians parenting

http://www.scholastic.com/MagicSchoolBus/index.html — Magic School Bus

http://nch.ari.net/education/ — National Coalition for the Homeless

http://www.nativeauthors.com/ — Native American authors

http://www.native@ipl.org — Native American authors

http://indy4.fdl.cc.mn.us/~isk/books/bookmenu.html — Native American books

http://www.pitt.edu/~imitten/indians.html — Native American groups & festivals

http://www.harpercollins.com/kids/ — Offers a wide variety of information

http://www.youth.org/loco/personproject/resources — Overcoming homophobia in the classroom

http://www.rethingingschools.org — Rethinking Schools journal

http://place.scholastic.com/ — Scholastic Place, Contests, projects, electronic publications and an online education store

http://place.scholastic.com/goosebumps/index.htm — Scholastic's Goosebumps

http://www.swarthmore.edu/~sjohnson/stories/ — Stories and storytellers

http://www.technet.com/ — Teacher's Edition Online

http://www.pacificnet.net/~mandel/ — Teachers Helping Teachers

http://www.cldc.howard.edu/~neca/cataloq.html — Teaching for Change Catalog

http://www.disney.com — Walt Disney books

http://www.ucalgary.ca/~dkbrown/index.html — Web Guide all aspects of children's books

http://wakko.exo.com/sassinak/pooh.html — Winnie the Pooh Resource Page